Breaking Free from the Chains of Role Ascriptions

Martina Lackner

Breaking Free from the Chains of Role Ascriptions

From Female Powerlessness to Powerful Solutions in Career, Partnership and Family

Martina Lackner
cross m – consulting studies & marketing
Eltville am Rhein, Germany

ISBN 978-3-658-43838-8   ISBN 978-3-658-43839-5 (eBook)
https://doi.org/10.1007/978-3-658-43839-5

Translation from the German language edition: "Raus aus dem Regiment der Rollenzuschreibungen" by Martina Lackner © Der/die Herausgeber bzw. der/die Autor(en), exklusiv lizenziert durch Springer Fachmedien Wiesbaden 2023. Published by Springer Berlin Heidelberg. All Rights Reserved.

This book is a translation of the original German edition "Raus aus dem Regiment der Rollenzuschreibungen" by Martina Lackner, published by Springer Fachmedien Wiesbaden GmbH in 2023. The translation was done with the help of an artificial intelligence machine translation tool. A subsequent human revision was done primarily in terms of content, so that the book will read stylistically differently from a conventional translation. Springer Nature works continuously to further the development of tools for the production of books and on the related technologies to support the authors.

© The Editor(s) (if applicable) and The Author(s), under exclusive license to Springer Fachmedien Wiesbaden GmbH, part of Springer Nature 2024

This work is subject to copyright. All rights are solely and exclusively licensed by the Publisher, whether the whole or part of the material is concerned, specifically the rights of translation, reprinting, reuse of illustrations, recitation, broadcasting, reproduction on microfilms or in any other physical way, and transmission or information storage and retrieval, electronic adaptation, computer software, or by similar or dissimilar methodology now known or hereafter developed.
The use of general descriptive names, registered names, trademarks, service marks, etc. in this publication does not imply, even in the absence of a specific statement, that such names are exempt from the relevant protective laws and regulations and therefore free for general use.
The publisher, the authors, and the editors are safe to assume that the advice and information in this book are believed to be true and accurate at the date of publication. Neither the publisher nor the authors or the editors give a warranty, expressed or implied, with respect to the material contained herein or for any errors or omissions that may have been made. The publisher remains neutral with regard to jurisdictional claims in published maps and institutional affiliations.

This Springer imprint is published by the registered company Springer Fachmedien Wiesbaden GmbH, part of Springer Nature.
The registered company address is: Abraham-Lincoln-Str. 46, 65189 Wiesbaden, Germany

Paper in this product is recyclable.

"The female career path, leading to women in positions of power, still seems to be far from a given even today."

However, it is up to women to question concepts such as power and powerlessness for themselves and individually, and to examine their own life path as well as decisions already made or still pending with self-honesty. Ms. Lackner guides the readers through the individual stages of life, from early childhood imprinting by parents and environment to later partnership, and makes it clear that the combination of partnership, motherhood, and career can still be akin to an act of juggling today. She offers a selection of options that can help ensure that women do not lose themselves in daily tasks and responsibilities.

The book illustrates that a woman must start with herself in order to initiate larger changes in the world by living her life authentically and honestly.

Dr. Viktoria Kickinger, Supervisory Board Member and Entrepreneur.

Foreword

In 2021, according to the Federal Statistical Office, just under a third of women worked in German executive suites. In the EU-wide ranking of the 27 member states, this was a shameful 20th place. And: In the past ten years, the proportion of female executives has hardly evolved.

So, if one asks why—in contrast to many other countries—there are still so few women in leadership positions in Germany, or why there are so many unbalanced and therefore often unhappy relationships, the answer of this book is: The cause primarily lies in the life stories of these women, in their unconscious images and fears. The book illuminates why many women do not develop professionally as they could, and/or fall into a dependent situation in a partnership or marriage, which does not support their professional development, and it shows ways out.

For me, the path to dependency and self-exploitation begins early: Fairy tales still perpetuate the image of the prince who makes the girl a queen or rescues her from an evil spell. In these young years, there are hardly any images of independent girls who develop their own goals and go their own way. However, even young girls should set the goal of taking their lives into their own hands, becoming financially independent, and not waiting for "their prince". When choosing their profession, young women should not primarily let the compatibility of career and family decide, but above all their own interests and abilities, and not least the remuneration.

Having one's own income, sufficient to secure a livelihood, and allowing for flexibility, means co-determination and co-creation for women, especially when a couple becomes a family and the distribution of family tasks needs to be regulated. The moment a young woman receives her education for a well-paid profession, she learns what is needed for professional advancement. Much of this is also important in a partnership: articulating and defending one's own desires, finding compromises, and—yes—also exercising power to shape something. She then also learns that one can fail and needs a "Plan B". She becomes the maker of her life, both professionally and privately. She is not afraid to assume and demand power, often an unconscious obstacle to advancement in hierarchies. She enjoys shaping things, her thinking space expands. Although this woman can still make a wrong choice in a partner due to the unconscious mechanisms described in this book, it is then easier to escape from an unfavorable connection.

No question: Not every woman will succeed in getting a high-paying job. But even then, it is important to articulate desires in both the partnership and the profession, to be able to interact on an equal footing, and above all to become aware of the deeply ingrained images and fears that obstruct a free path.

Aren't we all the architects of our own fortune?

Prof. Helga Rübsamen-Schaeff

Greetings from Supporters

The new normal of the powerful woman
For more than ten years, we at Feminess have been supporting women in achieving their professional goals. In doing so, we repeatedly encounter the same challenges, which align precisely with the theses of this book: At its core, it's always about giving oneself permission, the permission to be successful in one's career, the permission to break through dogmas that govern the role of women, the permission to realize oneself professionally and privately, without constantly feeling guilty.

The role assignment in Germany is still very present, even if it is covered by the cloak of gender equality. Recently, I was horrified to witness a debate about the membership of women in the shooting club. The shooting club is just a synonym for the traditional culture of excluding women from male domains.

Since it is still not a matter of course to grant women their rightful position in society in every way, I consider this work by Martina Lackner to be a must-read—for all women who are not satisfied with the status quo!

And the first step for any woman who strives for more success and fulfillment in her life is to become aware of her own power. Every time I talk about power at my events, the audience divides into two camps. One half vehemently rejects power as a term and sees it as something negative. The other half understands power as something to be fought for, and they are ready to "step into the ring" for it.

Yet power is neither something that should be rejected, nor something that should incite struggle. Power is initially a neutral, even self-evident part of the interplay between man and woman. Everything that follows the term power are our own evaluations. What if we women are powerful beings from birth, who stand up for themselves, their needs, and their professional advancement with absolute self-evidence? What would change in society if we acknowledge our power and shape our lives according to our own needs? Would we then succumb to the negative power games or would we rise above them and do what we really want? Would we persist in a job whose conditions undermine our power and keep us permanently small? Would we continue to allow role assignments that conform to the norm, even though we do not agree with them, and even reject them in part?

I am sure we would not! For this reason, I can only recommend this book to every ambitious woman, to consciously break through role models and to recognize and live their own power again. I wish you wonderful insights and deep changes with this reading.
Marina Henze, founder and owner of Feminess

Power makes feminine
Women and power or powerful women: two terms that are rarely mentioned together. Power is still too often defined as male in our society. Because in most key positions in our society, such as in politics and economics, men sit who defend these powerfully. Obviously, qualification alone does not count. Instead, laws and rules are needed to bring about changes and break up existing structures, because the path to the top for women, no matter how well educated they may be, seems to be more difficult. When women manage to take a position of power, they have a long, strenuous "male" fight behind them—which quickly

generates the image of the masculine woman when it comes to leadership. Female bosses, female in the classic and conventional sense, is that possible? Yes!

Power is not just the status at the end of the food chain—power is also the ability to inspire, lead, and bring about decisions. It refers to the ability to influence the thinking and behavior of individuals and groups in order to achieve success. Something that women master fabulously.

Let's return to the initial situation and ask ourselves: Why are men more powerful or able to exert their power more effectively and attain coveted professional positions? Why does it still seem difficult to develop an understanding of the power and strength of women and to bring about corresponding changes?

Women have power, as Martina Lackner clearly demonstrates in her book. However, the awareness of their own strength is lacking. The use of power is also unfamiliar to many women. For centuries, women have been fighting for equality, respect, and participation. But it is only with legal regulations that this is recognized and perceived. We praise our power to have achieved something after a successful conclusion, and forget that we have actually carried this power within us all along. So what can we do to get out of this seemingly powerless position? How can we finally become aware of our power and strength—and, once we are aware of it, find the courage to use and apply it to our advantage? And not just within the familiar confines of our own four walls.

Too often, women still grow up with the outdated beliefs that we all know, which are unnecessary to quote here. Therefore, the first step is to become aware of our power and overcome the fear of our own power.

Therefore, my passionate appeal to all women: Be brave, trust in your strength, and make power feminine!

Carolin Schäufele, editor of the women's career magazine *SHE works!*

Dear Readers!

The proportion of women in the executive suites of German companies is still low. While it was at 14.4% in the management of listed companies in 2022, it was only 8.3% in German family businesses. More than two-thirds of large family businesses do not have a single woman in top management (Source: Allbright Foundation). Even though the legislator prescribes a minimum share of women in the board and management with the Leadership Positions Act II, the path to equality at all levels is still long. So much for the facts.

What politics, economy, and society tell us women is always the same narrative, only in different shades and nuances. When a new law comes into effect, such as the introduction of quotas, positive reports are made about progress in companies and negative ones when some companies strictly refuse to bring women into top leadership positions. The narrative always goes in one direction: politics is doing too little and companies lack interest. However, one can, and this is where I see my task, also look at the topic from another side: women have power, but they do not use it. Because they do not know it, do not allow themselves to reach for power, or are afraid of power.

As a psychologist, psychological psychotherapist, and systemic coach, I have spent many years in coaching, in publications based on interviews with female managers, and most recently in a qualitative psychological study on the career obstacles of highly qualified women, dealing with the psyche of women and their intrapsychic factors such as motivation and resistance.

The psychological study "Side by Side" from 2020 illuminates complex (behavioral) psychological and subconsciously acting phenomena, thereby uncovering taboo topics. Because the thematic starting point is the families of origin of women with career potential. My colleagues and I have examined both the choice of partner and one's own lifestyle with and without children, as well as the question of professional desire and personal ambition against the background of blocking or supporting experiences from the subjects' own families of origin—women between 25 and 55 years old who still want to make a career, on the way up or already there. At the same time, the study is dedicated to the reality in German companies: the experienced leadership everyday life, the existing adversities and experiences made on the way up. The insights gained are the basis for this book.

Conclusion of the study: Women are more or less in the process of adapting to their partner, family, and job. They allow themselves little to no room to assume their own, especially emotionally independent position. Even if they appear to be successful in their careers, they remain in a victim status. They do not allow themselves to seize power (with one exception: in the family context), but remain in the role assigned to them. Based on this knowledge, I have developed recommendations for action for women:

- For young women who are faced with the decision to embark on career paths, deal with the choice of a partner, or with the topic: to have a child or not to have a child?
- for women who are already on their way to or in leadership positions and are confronted with obstacles by partners, colleagues, and superiors, or who want to learn more about the potential minefields of their environment, both professionally and privately,

- For women who are trying to navigate the balancing act between husband, child, and career, women who possess a high intrinsic motivation to develop further, both professionally and personally, who are not afraid to look into the mirror that this book provides, women who are ready to work on themselves and negotiate with their husband, colleagues, or bosses, women for whom children do not represent a retreat from their career.

In short: This book is aimed at women who dare to make bold decisions, speak plainly, and break free from role assignments.

I share with you my knowledge about partly conscious, partly unconscious behaviors, strategies, and emotions of women. My advice is not always nice, but is intended to stimulate you to think, to question your own patterns, and to draw consequences from them. I am a mirror for you: I analyze you, but at the same time show you possible ways out of your situation. If my findings and advice provoke resistance or even anger, it could be that I have hit a sore point. You can then pursue your anger or resistance or put the book aside. Some of my recommendations I live myself or have lived in my past. Therefore, I can assure you: They work within the framework of what you have in hand. Which brings me to the actual goal of this book:

I want to empower you to become the "maker" of your life or to develop in that direction. You have more power than you think, you just use it too little or not at all! Or you use it where it does not advance your career. Because the power of women is not least thwarted by millennia-old traditions and biological dispositions. Physical burdens such as pregnancy, childbirth, menstrual cycles, and menopause weaken women in their exercise of power. To come into their own power, women must confront their history and learn to understand connections in order to be able to break out of role assignments.

How is the book to be read?

The book begins with German history and a theoretical psychological background. In the subsequent chapters, I have repeatedly incorporated theoretical knowledge so that you can understand the connections: between German history and your own, the development of self-esteem, the significance of the family of origin, the criteria by which you choose a partner, how the decision to have children impacts your career, and last but not least, how the corporate system influences your decision for or against a career. In the individual chapters, I reflect theoretical knowledge for you and provide recommendations for action to challenge existing patterns and present solutions.

In this book, I openly address those taboo topics that subtly resonate in the discussion about women's quotas and women's promotion, about career women and bad mothers, but are not publicly recognized, named, and acknowledged. However, they are the key to women's power—and to breaking away from traditional role assignments.

The tips that each chapter contains only capture a part of the possible conclusions that can be useful for you as a reader. Because every woman has an individual story, associated themes, and inner resistances. It is impossible to cover everything in this book. Furthermore, I want to clarify: For the sake of simplicity, I speak of male and female stereotypes and, as an example, of a heteronormative relationship. That life and people are more diverse is undisputed.

In addition, you will find comments from female experts and leaders who enrich my texts at appropriate places with their own stories or expertise. The pictures I draw of both genders may fully, only partially, or hardly apply to you. There are numerous shades when it comes to the family of origin. The sketches are stereotypical, of course, reality is even more multifaceted and nuanced. I exaggerate conditions in this book to make them clearer. My sketches are intended to serve as a basis for discussions and to stimulate thought. You will occasionally encounter redundancies in my explanations. These are intentional, as I illuminate aspects from multiple perspectives and stages of life, into which the same factors sometimes come into play. One more note on gendering: I refrain from mentioning both gender forms in designations, even when I address both, and limit myself to the masculine form.

My declared goal: Out of powerlessness, into power! Become a powerful woman, so that you can meet your partner, boss, or other powerful people on an equal footing. And role assignments lose their effect.

Eltville am Rhein, Germany   Martina Lackner
June 2023

Acknowledgment

My greatest thanks go to my colleagues, Doris Manthei, Edith Pamminger, and Marianne Brandt, who conducted the side-by-side study with me. Without their psychological-therapeutic expertise and practical knowledge based on many years of experience, this book would not exist.

Thanks to my dear friend, Prof. Helga-Rübsamen Schaeff, who stood by my side as a preface writer and has become a real role model for me over the years.

Thanks also to Marina Friess from Feminess and Carolin Schäufele from *SHE works!*, who support this book project. Marina Friess has shown in a grandiose way with her further education offers for women how to move masses of women and create a special spirit. And Carolin Schäufele has created with *SHE works!* a career magazine for women that puts comprehensive, technically sound career focuses in the foreground.

I would also like to thank all those commentators and test readers, friends and network partners, who have given the book its diversity through their expert knowledge and long-standing experience as female leaders, coaches, trainers, and authors. It has become diverse thanks to them.

Last but not least, I would like to thank Petra Sonntag, who has accompanied my journalistic works with her editorial eye and has added spice to this book.

The Commentators

Mag. Edith Pamminger
As a clinical and health psychologist, as well as a systemic individual, couple, and family therapist, her daily work involves empowering and encouraging women in their resources and potentials to follow their own path. Ms. Mag. Pamminger assists them in recognizing their own strengths, desires, and needs, and in progressing on their own path professionally and personally despite resistance, stereotypes, and role expectations.
https://praxis-webergasse.at

Marianne Brandt
Entrepreneur and has been active as a coach and organizational developer for 30 years, and has engaged in conversation with more than 2500 women on the path to self-realization.
https://www.raum-fuer-entwicklung.com/marianne-brandt.html

Doris Manthei
Her career journey has made her an expert in the field of career and life planning for women. As the managing director of a non-profit

organization, a systemic family therapist, and coach, Doris Manthei has worked with and for women over many years, establishing institutions and accumulating diverse knowledge about their life trajectories, stumbling blocks, and barriers—and how to successfully overcome them. As a systemic thinker through and through, she finds it easy to recognize patterns of behavior, identify existing resources, and suggest solutions. Her motto for strong, authentic women and those who aspire to be: She came, she saw, she conquered.

Dr. Ursula Koehler

The PhD pharmacist Dr. Ursula Koehler is a person who navigates life with a great deal of pace and decision-making joy. After more than 18 years on the national and international pharmaceutical scene, she now indulges her passion for interpersonal relationships with a focus on personal development and leadership, alongside her scientific precision. Her own experiences consistently flow into her work as an author, speaker, and coach. In addition to leadership responsibilities, she personally strives to empower women and particularly mothers, assisting them in finding and pursuing their own path with clarity, courage, and joy.
www.ursulakoehler.de

Daniela Mündler

The economist has made a career in renowned consumer goods and trading companies, among others as a board member of Bahlsen GmbH & Co. KG in Hanover. The married mother of three children has articulated her claim to leadership early in her professional development and is now pursuing it with the founding of her own company. She has been volunteering since 2008 in the women's network Generation CEO e. V., since 2018 as a member of the board. She is a mentor, advisory board member, and senior advisor for various organizations.

Dr. Angelika Weinländer-Mölders

The doctoral chemist has more than 20 years of leadership expertise at C-level in the life science and chemistry environment. She has been a long-standing member of the Seedfinancing Board of the Austria Wirtschafts Service, which handles the PreSeed and Seedfinancing of start-ups for the Austrian Ministry of Economics. Dr. Angelika Weinländer-Mölders is a co-editor and author of the book *21 Successful Women—21 Career Formulas* as well as the book *Men at the Side of Successful Women—Side by Side to the Top*.

Michaela Kay
She has held leadership roles as a manager, managing director, and board member in international companies for over 20 years and is currently an independent lawyer, particularly as a consultant and board member. As a mother of two children, she is familiar with the associated challenges. She advises and supports companies and individuals in crisis and conflict situations, as well as in the design and implementation of change processes. In doing so, she primarily works in a relationship-oriented manner for a change in the culture of cooperation and for greater diversity in society and organizations.

Theresa Nerz
She studied Life Sciences and completed her Master's in Biotechnology in 2022—she is therefore ready to ascend the career ladder. In addition to the natural sciences, the social media sector, among other things through her work in the btS-Life Sciences Student Initiative e. V., has become an area in which she has expertise.

Editorial Accompaniment
Petra Sonntag has accompanied the study and this book as a freelance journalist and copywriter—with enthusiasm for the topic, a critical eye on text comprehension and readability, and a passion for the well-written word. She has been working as an editor on both sides of the desk, in public relations as well as in traditional journalism, since 2006, dedicating herself to a variety of topics and formats.
    https://das-wort-von-sonntag.de

Contents

1   **On the Power and Roles of Men and Women**   1

2   **Where Do We Come from and What Does that Do to Us?**   7
- 2.1   Transgenerational Transmission   8
- 2.2   Development of Self-Worth and Ego-Strength   13
- 2.3   The Importance of the Family of Origin   18
- Literature   23

3   **The Power of Our Past and Origin**   25
- 3.1   Dysfunctional Family Constellations   28
  - 3.1.1   Unrelated Parents   28
  - 3.1.2   Dominant father and adapted mother   32
  - 3.1.3   Dominant Mother and Self-Insecure Father   35
  - 3.1.4   Competing Parents   38
  - 3.1.5   Insecure and Fearful Parents   42
- 3.2   Functional Family Constellations   44
- Literature   47

4   **When Hormones Take the Lead**   49
- Literature   53

5 The Balancing Act between Partnership, Motherhood, and Career — 55
- 5.1 Power at First Sight? — 59
- 5.2 Partnerships—from Career Supporters to Career Brakes — 60
  - 5.2.1 The Classic: Side by Side with the "Yes-but" Man — 60
  - 5.2.2 We are definitely not a team: Wrong partner choice and competitive relationships — 70
  - 5.2.3 The Ideal Case: "Honey, I'm in!"—The Couple as a Team — 74
- 5.3 Excursus: Partner Search and Motherhood — 77
  - 5.3.1 Partner Search on an Equal Footing — 77
  - 5.3.2 Motherhood and the Traps and Illusions of Women — 80
- 5.4 Excursion: Large Family Instead of Small Family — 95
- 5.5 Women and Their Side Stages: Girlfriend, Mother, Mother-in-law, and Network Partners — 98
- Literature — 104

6 Leadership in Conflict—Discrepancy between Desire and Reality — 105
- 6.1 High demand and blind spot—this is how women lead — 108
- 6.2 Covert or Secret Leadership — 113
  - 6.2.1 The Secret Boss — 113
  - 6.2.2 Leading Pleasurably in Secret — 114
- 6.3 The Denied Leadership Claim — 114
- 6.4 Renouncing Leadership as a Protective Measure — 115
- Literature — 116

7 Power and Powerlessness: The Experienced Leadership — 117
- 7.1 And Daily Greet Dogma, Dominance and Dismantling — 118
- 7.2 Career Break Motherhood? — 120

	7.3	Backgrounds for the Devaluation of Mothers by Superiors	123
	7.4	Lack of Personal Responsibility and Its Consequences	126
		Literature	128
8	**Principles of Violence in German Companies**	129
	8.1	Our Collective Heritage	129
	8.2	The Fear of Leadership of Competent Women	131
	8.3	The Consequence: Women Do Not Reach Their Full Power	132
	8.4	Women's Blind Spots as an Indication of Fear-Violence Spirals	133
	8.5	Burying the Hatchet	134
	8.6	The Brake Block Fear	136
		Literature	138
9	**Tools and Strategies for Dealing with Powerfully Aggressive People**	139
	9.1	How Do I Extricate Myself from Power-Impotence Relationships?	139
	9.2	Exiting Power-Impotence Spirals	143
10	**Conclusion**	149

Addendum   153

Glossary   155

Book Recommendations   161

About the Author

Psychologist, psychotherapist, author, and executive mentor for women in top positions and companies that have understood that they benefit from the full potential development of their top women. Martina Lackner joined a four-member team of experts in the fields of female identity and women's promotion, executive development, psychology, and systemic family and psychotherapy in 2019 to research career obstacles for women. The occasion was both her work as co-editor of the book *Men at the Side of Successful Women Side by Side to the Top* and the recurring question from HR managers as to why so few women want to go into leadership—despite internal women's promotion programs and diversity efforts in the company. Her slogan: Become powerful and influential with strategic skill.

www.martinalackner.com

1

On the Power and Roles of Men and Women

Abstract The common role attributions can only take hold as they still do because women do not use their own power enough. Often they lack self-esteem, they feel weak and powerless—and send corresponding signals of submission. Those who have their own power, on the other hand, signal authority and this ensures equality. The power issue becomes a topic in every relationship at some point: between partners, on the job between boss and employees, among colleagues, between parents and children, between friends, within women's networks, and between mother and daughter.

The common role assignments can only take hold as they still do because women do not use their own power enough. Often they lack self-esteem, they feel weak and powerless—and send corresponding signals of submission. Those who have their own power, on the other hand, signal authority and this ensures equality. The question of power becomes an issue in every relationship at some point: between partners, on the job between boss and employees, among colleagues, between parents and children, between friends, within women's networks, and between mother and daughter.

Within couple relationships, there is a constant balancing and rebalancing of a power relationship that repeatedly falls out of balance. Couples on an equal footing, who have the same values and goals, are less affected by this imbalance. In couple relationships where the man is still patriarchally influenced and has conservative ideas about his partner's career, the pendulum in the power relationship will swing in favor of the man. Because he will try to assert himself—either until he has her where he wants her, or the relationship breaks down, from both sides.

While men in relationships that follow traditional role assignments secure their power through income, status, and career, women exercise their power in such relationships through shared children, eroticism, and attractiveness. They adapt their behavior to the role assigned to them. But adaptation is nothing more than a process of denial. This denial often leads to latent aggressions—towards the partner, the children, or other women who refuse the role assignment. Behind the denial are shame, guilt, and fears. A huge emotional obstacle to personal development, needs, and desires.

So it is essentially about the question of self-empowerment: How can one become more powerful in order to be recognized as equal, in the job, but also in private life?

> "Power in itself is, in my eyes, neutral and nothing more than often granted strength or empowerment to shape, make decisions, and take responsibility. So it depends on how and for what you use it. Strengthening and self-empowerment mean standing up for your own needs and perceiving your own healthy boundaries and communicating them. Many people have a problem with power, especially women. We equate power with control, violence, aggression, and other things that we usually find as power abuse in hierarchical structures."
> Michaela Kay, consultant and board member.

When you ask women if they aspire to powerful positions in corporate structures, some will wave it off. Because they do not allow themselves power, are afraid of it, or fear overburdening. An overburdening that arises because they have to fight for power in the existing structures and then defend it. Apart from the fact that they have rarely made it into outstanding power positions until the introduction of the quota, few women aspire to power.

They are interested in technical content, in democratic decisions in the team, in value orientation, but hardly in leading others powerfully and taking sole responsibility. Power seems to be something dirty that one should not aspire to as a woman. On the one hand, this is based on messages like "Power is not for you". And on the other hand, the system-immanent over- and subordination in the hierarchical context of a company creates an environment that facilitates power abuse. The mostly male role models who exercise and often abuse power are not suitable for women as orientation. Women cannot identify with this because fights and conflicts usually diametrically oppose their value system. The idea that power also has a positive character, e.g., in the form of shaping power in leadership positions, is not anchored in women, nor is the idea of self-empowerment, namely allowing oneself to become more powerful and powerful—first of all, to get on an equal footing.

Women are not used to seizing power. They have few role models or those that are far removed from their own reality. Especially for young girls, the existence of stars on TikTok seems much more desirable than a female chancellor. Even their own mother is not really a role model for many women. Why should she be? The mothers' generation of today's 40-year-olds, who could now move up into management, were raised by mothers who themselves made little or no careers and were not on an equal footing with their men in the partnership. This generation has already made it further than their mothers, many of them were able to complete a degree, but how to reconcile child and career, there is no template from their own family for this.

So what do women who aspire to power against this background do? They look for a terrain that is easiest for them to conquer because there are blueprints for it: the power over their own children and over some partners! There has always been a shift in women's power interests in the family context.

The fact that women give up on careers or withdraw from a certain level is also based on the fact that they live out their lust for power on a different stage. This stage is much less dangerous for them: they do not expect to be fired, their career does not stop, but they also do not receive a bonus. They are satisfied with the power over their children and often their own partner.

> "It seems strange to claim that women exercise their power in the family... even here, this is often not seen as power, but as 'I can/know better'. The fact that this represents a claim to power is usually in the realm of blind spots."
> Marianne Brandt, coach and organizational developer.

Hand on heart: Who decides who is invited to the Christmas celebration? Who controls and regulates the leisure behavior of the adolescent daughter? Who checks the homework and even the teachers? Who decides where to go on vacation? And who tries to secure special treats by being accommodating on certain nights? And many a woman also supports her husband emotionally. The care work does not end with the children, but often with her own husband, who may be good at his job, but to be good in life, needs a woman who listens to him, coaches him, prepares food for him, and prepares him for meetings because she can better empathize with the sensitivities of bosses and colleagues. She does all this without pay.

The power that women exercise is intertwined. The aggression that women also have in connection with lust for power must not be openly lived out, so only secretly or it is suppressed. Suppressed aggressions come as poisoned arrows, "the bitch" or "the fury" is then said or they result in depressions.

Women live in self-denial and in fear of openly grasping for power. Therefore, they turn away from the company or do not strive for leadership positions, become dependent on the partner and thus harm themselves—and thus also do not contribute to a transformation of the system.

> "'That women do all this is self-evident.' I have often heard this sentence from women. Anyone who lives or wants to live a different role model, who demands 'compensation' in the intra-family context for it, is considered crazy, impudent or... by both men and women. The headwind is accompanied by a growing portion of self-doubt."
> Marianne Brandt, coach and organizational developer.

Grasping for powerful positions is not desired, neither by one's own partner nor by companies. And there are only a few role models for this. Women are not trained to take over leadership and often take the easier and probably less conflict-ridden path via the family. Added to this is the testosterone-driven and aggressively charged behavior of male executives, which is very competitive. This behavior scares women. They want to lead differently.

> "Women devote themselves for a while to the growing up of the children and the advancement of the man. This role carries temporarily, nourishes self-confidence, makes satisfied and creates meaning. But the children grow up, become adults, go their own ways. If there is no edifying professional standing, it leads to loss of identity and—if the partnership is no longer viable—inevitably to a crisis of meaning or to psychosomatic complaints up to psychological crises. Starting a career at 50 then becomes really difficult. I know such case histories from my psychological practice."
> Edith Pamminger, clinical and health psychologist, systemic psychotherapist.

I could tell you at this point like many other advisors and coaches: Become braver and more resilient, try it out! But I don't think much of such advice. How do you tell a woman to grasp for power when she has a deep-seated problem with it and female leadership does not arrive in a patriarchal system? Either the system has to change or the women, preferably both. However, this represents a more than difficult task, for both sides.

I find it worrying that content, technicality, and values are neglected because the more dominant ones in this system prevail—for the sake of prevailing. It is just as worrying that women shy away from leadership positions because they fear dominance, and prefer to stay in the family comfort zone, while their husbands and life partners seek the "battlefield business". At this point, both sides are challenged. We need men *and* women in leadership positions, because both genders combine in combination characteristics that promise maximum success: the assertiveness of men and their striving for more and the high technical competence of women, coupled with a value system. Unfortunately, we are still in an antagonism. We have not learned to combine the advantages of both genders to achieve maximum success. We only know the model: If one prevails, the other must automatically lose or give in, because this is (unfortunately) the classic hierarchical model of our coexistence, in private as well as in professional context.

The fact is that women adapt in such systems, often give in in couple relationships, let themselves be "softened" and give men the lead. In the company, they wage a half-hearted battle for leadership positions. A few women, board members and managers, have had a rocky road behind them and have managed to assert themselves in a male-dominated environment. The rest of the women are neither so combative nor do they have the right partner or the intrinsic motivation—it is a conglomerate of various factors. However, they all have one factor in common: They lack an adequate way of dealing with the power and aggression of men, both privately and professionally. They find it difficult to counteract this. Because women have hardly learned in their history to get on an equal footing with men. This only works if you do not let yourself be overpowered, but negotiate, demand your rights, defend your position sustainably and determinedly or simply keep your hands off power people. And not wait for men to grant women rights!

Women are also under illusions: They think that if they conform and submit to the powerful side, they will benefit from it. This is only partially true. Women who conform have to achieve a lot to gain respect and recognition. They expend themselves over long distances and in the end, it is questionable whether the reward really compensates them.

So how do women come into their own power and on an equal footing with powerful men? In order to be able to "opt out" of the regime of role attributions. Because the development of personal power is directly and immediately related to the effect of role attributions. I will try to answer this central question in the individual chapters.

2

Where Do We Come from and What Does that Do to Us?

Abstract Transgenerational transmissions, the development of self-esteem and ego strength, as well as growing up in a functional family of origin, significantly influence the power development of women—and either slow it down, prevent it, or promote it. This developmental history forms the basis for healthy power behavior and a critical approach to role attributions.

The power development of women has always been and almost without exception been slowed down in every society. The distortion begins with the fact that women are denied any striving for power. And they hardly have any. Whether they strive for power, they usually cannot answer themselves, because every attempt at it has been nipped in the bud and still is. Various psychological explanatory models provide insight into the power development in women.

At the beginning of the unequal treatment of women and their perceived or actual powerlessness is a story that often leads to women's silence. The story of women and their ancestors, the story of their people, and a personal story. This triad largely determines the emotional experience of women—how they feel as women, how they shape and experience relationships with men and their children, and last but not least, how they build and manage relationships with colleagues and superiors, whether they aspire to leadership positions or reject them, and how they develop and unfold their own power.

Women, like men, always carry their history with them: a backpack filled with beliefs, attitudes, and above all fears, insecurities, humiliations, and emotional pain.

> "Men are usually shaped by their mothers, by their values and female role understanding. This would be an opportunity for women to raise their sons more openly and gender-neutrally."
> Edith Pamminger, clinical and health psychologist, systemic psychotherapist.

Join me on a journey into the world of transgenerational transmissions. Learn what contributes to the development of self-strength, self-esteem, and self-confidence, and the importance of your family of origin. So that you can understand how you have become the woman you are today, why you have become this way, and what consequences this has for your personal and professional life path.

2.1 Transgenerational Transmission

The Curse of the Past
It is important to become aware of the impact of the past. A look back at the past centuries and what women have experienced: witch burning, rapes, lawlessness, death in childbirth, then two world wars, for which Germany was largely responsible. This experience has an impact on subsequent generations. In technical terms, this phenomenon is referred to as transgenerational transmission processes, which I have examined in more detail together with my colleagues Marianne Brandt, Doris Manthei, and Edith Pamminger in the Side-by-Side study (2020): Transgenerational transmissions mean that severe experiences

of violence by perpetrators and victims cause traumas that continue to manifest themselves in subsequent generations. Freud referred to this process as "emotional inheritance". In psychotherapy, this phenomenon can have an effect over several generations, as an example from the practice of Edith Pamminger shows:

> **Example**
> "A woman came to me in therapy with a severe anxiety disorder, although there were no parameters in this direction in her life. She led a content, carefree life. In therapy, it turned out that her grandparents were murdered in a concentration camp, her parents had never worked through this, and unconscious fears had been passed on to the children."
> Edith Pamminger, clinical and health psychologist, systemic psychotherapist.

Even though other countries and people were also heavily traumatized by wars, one can still derive a national specificity from its history in Germany. Germany was twice a perpetrator nation and war loser in a short period of time. At the end of the wars, the Germans primarily saw themselves as victims—because of the demands for reparations by the victorious powers, the severe famine as a result of the war, the arbitrary rule suffered under the Nazis, widespread bombings of the civilian population leading to the destruction of cities, as well as the rapes and murders of women and children (Source: Brandt et al. 2020).

And what does this mean for women?
If we pursue the question of why the process of equal treatment of women, especially the parity occupation of leadership positions, is tough and much discussed, this question is closely related to German history, which I explain with my colleagues in the Side-by-Side study: It is a special mixture of deep-seated and blocking shame, guilt, overestimation, and denial that continues to have an effect in Germany and also manifests itself in subsequent generations, among other things, in the form of obedience, the establishment of taboos, deep-seated (failure) fears, radicalization, or the admiration of human hardness in all areas of our social and economic life. The result is that both men and women

dissociate from feelings and fulfill predefined roles behind which both genders hide—emotionless and adapting to the respective predefined role model. But behind the facade of a role, a function, or even expertise, personalities fade, they appear hollow.

> "For me, this is also a reason why, if you personally live a different role model, you encounter an uncomprehending environment and are immediately excluded from society. People who dare to be different still have a hard time with us. Whether it's a relationship on an equal footing or simply a very tolerant open attitude towards life—deviating from common role attributions arouses a suspicious feeling in the majority."
>
> Dr. Angelika Weinländer-Mölders, chemist, manager, and co-editor of *Side by side—Men at the side of successful women*.

Our conclusion: Both genders are still subject to the pull of their parents' or grandparents' generation's traumas. The usual leadership habitus still seems to orient itself towards the supposedly strong man. Women often prefer to stay in the second row, even though their skills and their special system relevance—in the job as well as in the family—are undisputed.

In addition, both genders have a high need for security regarding their identity. They are therefore tempted to preserve traditional behavior and fulfill the role assignments inscribed therein. This phenomenon occurs on both a conscious and unconscious level: men seek power and expect obedience, women adapt. This is in stark contrast to the fact that more women than men have better educational and professional qualifications, marriages no longer guarantee security and stability, and both men and women now have to provide for the family income.

Male dominance and female willingness to adapt are two stereotypes that still have their firm place in society and the economy. They are fueled by the fear and guilt entanglements of our history, which continues in this way: fears and feelings of guilt are passed on and shape coexistence. For women, it is the fear of male violence, which in the 21st century is only disguised and subtle in both companies and partnerships. It is therefore not immediately recognizable as such. "However, some forms of male violence are very obvious," says Edith Pamminger, clinical and health psychologist, systemic psychotherapist. She refers to data from the umbrella organization of autonomous women's shelters in Austria: "In Austria in 2022, about three women were murdered every month until September. In the majority of femicides, there was a relationship or family relationship between the perpetrator and the victim. In the current year 2022, an estimated 24 women have already been murdered" (Source: https://www.aoef.at).

In German offices, no one is beaten (see Chap. 8). On the contrary: If you believe the press releases from companies, they do a lot for women. Diversity is the buzzword of the hour. Flags in rainbow colors are also flying everywhere, and the social media posts of companies give the impression that diversity and compatibility are the focus of their actions. The political pressure is high. But if you take a look behind the facades of the company headquarters and talk to employees, a different picture emerges.

> "Companies are lying to themselves and others. Because making our system more diverse means a profound transformation based on a new understanding, which requires an individual willingness for development and a change in meaning and culture. It is indeed desired that women adapt to the current system, but not that the entire system is transformed. In this respect, diversity efforts are often more about clinging to the existing than opening up to something new."
> Michaela Kay, consultant and board member.

Those who look more closely get the impression that German companies are secretly in a state of war or in a hierarchical state of rigidity. Opponents can always be found if needed: the competitor, the customer, the service provider, the women and often also male employees, if they do not fit into the concept of the decision-makers. The motto seems to be: everyone against everyone. In the fight for the resource of leadership position, the resource of profit and bonuses, or the resource of attention and image, the stronger one will prevail. The means of this fight are open and hidden aggressions, belittling and softening people (e.g., by excluding them from meetings, mail distribution lists, assignment of leadership positions), bullying, pronounced control behavior, dominance behavior up to choleric outbursts of managers, to name just a few characteristics of the war. By the way, these behaviors are not only observed in men, but increasingly also in women in leadership positions. Microaggressions are therefore not just a domain of men. Women also learn from the habitus of male bosses and colleagues when they rise hierarchically and have the opportunities to do so.

> "Distrust is a central driver. The motto of my father (born 1940) was: Trust no one with the thoughts of your heart. Today he is your friend and tomorrow he will falter."
> Dr. Ursula Koehler, systemic coach and expert for self-empowerment.

In partnerships, a similar picture emerges. Companies form an image of society with their staff. If we assume a secret battlefield in companies, this is fed by the people who come together there in a group. These people usually live in relationships in private. The difference: In the company they adapt to the system, in the private sphere their own rules apply—here they show their true *I*. And in the context of transgenerational transmissions for partnerships, this means: Here men act who strive to assert themselves, and women who adapt.

But many people, especially women and Generation Z, are no longer interested in a battlefield and obedience. Especially Generation Z is not as heavily burdened in the context of transgenerational transmissions as previous generations. They have enough distance from the traumas of the grandparents or great-grandparents generation. Divorces today not only occur because this option exists and the dissolution of a marriage is no longer sanctioned by society, but because women are now looking for partnerships on an equal footing and only a few men are able to live this equality, to share household and child rearing fairly, and to contribute to giving women freedom for their own career paths.

Diverse Levels of Change and the Personal Level as a Blind Spot

It is not enough to consider individual levels, problem areas, or relationships in isolation, for example, by focusing exclusively on external conditions through quota regulations for women or similar measures. A change towards more equality in the form of a balanced coexistence of male and female qualities can only succeed sustainably if we become aware of how complex this process is.

Change processes in this field affect various levels that need to be integrated. Change does not start with action, but with awareness, e.g., how deeply rooted

the structures of our millennia-old patriarchy are, externally and internally, i.e., within ourselves, in all our relationships, and especially within our families. This also necessary inner work is often a blind spot in this context. Inner change requires dealing with personal fears, beliefs, and injuries and recognizing how these shape our own behavior patterns.
Michaela Kay, Consultant and Board Member

2.2 Development of Self-Worth and Ego-Strength

The Impact of Our Personal History—A Significant Factor in Power Development
The following treatise on self-worth and ego-strength is taken from the Side-by-Side study (2020):

The way we lead ourselves in life, lead other people, or let ourselves be led, is largely formed in our childhood and adolescence, i.e., from our personal history. What we experience during this time and what messages we receive about our personality, what we want or have to believe ourselves, and how we have been recognized by our reference persons in our nature, shape our self-worth and our identity. With high self-worth, we can develop a positive ego-strength or, if our own value cannot be securely recognized by us, also a pseudo-ego-strength.

Often, we let ourselves be deceived by hierarchies and titles in our interactions, without suspecting what is happening psychologically in our counterpart. To better understand what drives us and others, it is worth looking at the foundations of our behaviors:

> **Self-Worth**
> Self-worth is the value we attribute to ourselves based on messages and experiences. Parents and other close reference persons shape our self-image and form the basis for the perception of our right to exist. This process of self-evaluation begins early in our life and is particularly shaped by the first two decades of life.

A positive/high self-worth develops when we were able to experience in childhood and adolescence that we are lovable and valuable, even with our personal weaknesses and mistakes. The willingness to perceive oneself with one's own strengths and weaknesses and to stand by them, to want to further develop one's own personality, as well as an open attitude in encounters with other people characterize good self-worth.

Feelings of inferiority as a sign of low self-worth arise exactly the opposite way, because these experiences were not made in earlier years and no benevolent attitude towards oneself and others has developed. The feeling of not being good enough and not being valuable means not having a secured right to exist on the inner psychological level. These people are insecure in their core nature and can quickly feel existentially threatened by other people or changed requirements.

Messages from Childhood
Most of us probably had the experience as a child of not being good enough, diligent, attractive, talented, neat, or disciplined. In the parental home and at school, there were constantly repeating messages from "above" that have ingrained themselves into our inner psychological mindset as drivers: "Try harder. Make something of yourself! Don't be so lazy, dreamy, playful, cheeky, rebellious!"—The list could be extended.

These experiences cannot simply be shrugged off, yet many of us as teenagers or young adults were able to establish a new balance of our self-image by adding successful experiences and positively overcome crises to personal ego-strengthening. Maturity and development also mean overcoming negative messages and experiences and developing one's own ego-identity and reliability.

Ego-Strength versus Pseudo-Ego-Strength
People with a well-developed, positive ego-strength can be recognized, for example, by their credible confidence in being able to find solutions even in unclear or unsettling situations. On the other hand, people with low ego-strength appear insecure to us, they tend to follow rather than take responsibility themselves. These people are not recommended for

2 Where Do We Come from and What Does that Do to Us?

special tasks or leadership positions. There is usually consensus about this within the system.

In addition to ego-strength, there is also the phenomenon of pseudo-ego-strength.

People with a pseudo-ego-strength can have a strong charisma and can bind masses of people to themselves with it. Many people attribute great leadership to them. The fact that these people can polarize extremely is interpreted by the followership at least as a special feature of their leadership competence. People with a pseudo-ego-strength have feelings of inferiority that are overcompensated. The desire for recognition, the overestimation of one's own abilities, and a lack of empathy are usually pronounced. It is typical for these personalities that they are extremely busy impressing others and soliciting admiration for themselves. They are not very capable of criticism and are extremely easily offended in their honor and self-understanding if they are not positively reinforced.

People with pseudo-self-strength have learned over many years to skillfully conceal their low self-esteem by hiding it behind a trained mask-like habitus. Internally, they feel completely different than they show externally. They stage a personality they would like to be, but can never be. A particular confusion also lies in the fact that these people make themselves believe that their external mask is actually their inner self-strength.

> "The eroding role attributions of the masculine over the past 40 years, accompanied by a loss of identity, intensify the insecurity. In conversations, two strategies for dealing with this are particularly noticeable: denial and instead continuing to 'pump up' and display dominance. Or 'pseudo-insight', which is shown by unpracticed reflection of one's own feelings, accompanied by speechlessness and discomfort, and leads to defensive behavior."
> Marianne Brandt, coach and organizational developer.

This type is particularly found in male-dominated top management—low self-esteem, equipped with a pseudo-self-strength, but protected and promoted by male peers. It is wrong to believe that low self-esteem or lack of self-strength only affects women. Men can hide behind a role: they were raised by some parents to be future princes and give themselves at least temporary support and security in the circle of men or let women do the work. At home, these men often hide behind their wives, they are emotionally held and secured by their partners. All these are reasons why men from dysfunctional family constellations (see Sect. 3.1) become more powerful and powerful than women. The deficits from the parental home do not weigh so heavily, they can be compensated more easily because the system supports them.

> "How wonderful it would have been if I had had this knowledge earlier. Then I would have left a company with a pseudo-self boss immediately and applied where a boss with real self-strength operates. Unfortunately, I didn't have a good antenna for this, it would have made my life easier and probably my career planning would have been simpler."
> Dr. Angelika Weinländer-Mölders, chemist, manager and co-editor of *Side by side—Men at the side of successful women.*

I can, I may, I want—the shortcoming of women

In people with a well-developed self-strength and at the same time good self-esteem, a positive consciousness in the sense of "I can, I may, I want" can develop: I can career, I may career and I want career. We attribute leadership and best career chances to truly self-confident and self-assured people. But it is precisely at this point that many women are lacking. While men are raised to not only be allowed to make a career, but they must (should) take on the role of the breadwinner because of their gender and the lack of self-esteem can be compensated, the "I can, may and want to make a career" in women is only very marginal and especially only up to a certain life phase.

This "I can, I may, I want" lasts in young women until graduation and through studies and then, until the biological clock ticks or/and they have reached a position in the company that they either experience as maximally achievable or also satisfying.

Here, between the ages of 30 and 40, there is a break, which can be attributed to various factors: With increasing advancement in the

2 Where Do We Come from and What Does that Do to Us?

company, there is a lack of confidence in one's own performance and existing competencies. Added to this are fears of failure and sometimes a desire to have children, accompanied by the fear of not being able to reconcile career and child. The lack of support from the partner and the impression of not being wanted as a woman in leadership positions also favor the break—not to mention the worry of having to survive on a secret battlefield.

> "Joy in self-reflection is good and important, and yet it can be too pronounced in women and then quickly overshoots the mark. Women are already prone to doubting themselves and their abilities and are not used to attributing special value to their abilities. They quickly feel like impostors ('imposter syndrome') and remain silent too often."
> Dr. Ursula Koehler, systemic coach and expert for self-empowerment.

When superiors, often male bosses in the patriarchal system, tell female top performers with performance and competence insecurities: "You still lack … on the way to becoming a leader" or "You are top, but …", then these women take such messages as an opportunity to work even harder because they finally want to be enough. A vicious circle.

Here begins the "I can, I may, I want" to crumble, it is in dissolution.

And at this point, women give up their power, the power over themselves. They remain true to the expectations of society, their superiors, their partner and environment, they adapt to the role attributions assigned to them—and lose themselves on their chosen path.

The self-worth and ego strength that young women have been able to build up in their biographies so far is not enough to naturally pursue their career path and to emancipate themselves in the private sphere in the context of household and childcare in such a way that they make demands on their partner to evenly distribute the burden of care work and domestic duties. Women rather adapt to their partner's ideas—to his understanding of roles, how to live child, household and partnership. They also adapt to societal ideas of how to live the mother role. And here, the prevailing opinion is still that "career women" are simply bad mothers—a term for which there is no equivalent in other languages. On a factual level, it is knockout arguments that employers and the personal environment bring to women: "How do you want to combine a leadership job with motherhood?" Or: "Whoever brings more money home has the right to more job. You surely want our child not to become conspicuous through all-day daycare."

Women cannot counter these statements. They react as their environment expects them to: with withdrawal or at least with remaining in a position or leadership position, with long absences due to parental leave, etc. With every decision they make for their life, they increasingly find themselves in a reactive and dependent position—towards the employer, the partner and also towards the children. In other words: They retreat into the traditional role description.

> "The cultural glue of adhering to the implicit rules subtly or directly influences women on many levels. Even if they have a supportive environment as a mother, it is extremely exhausting to assert oneself clearly and confidently in this spider web of resistance, well-intentioned advice, lack of daycare places or part-time leadership models etc. and one's own demands."
> Marianne Brandt, coach and organizational developer.

In addition to the experiences of violence that women and their ancestors have had, as well as the development of self-worth and ego strength, the family of origin plays a special role in the career of women: It is significantly involved in how women develop, especially their power, and behave in the social system and later in the company system. They reenact their own early experiences and emotional background—based on the relationships with the first reference persons father and mother.

2.3 The Importance of the Family of Origin

Unconscious Reenactments in Companies
The correlation between families of origin and educational opportunities, personal development opportunities or value concepts is well known to us. Less known is that emotions and learned behaviors from childhood and adolescence are unconsciously repeated as adults. Or in other words: As adults, experiences from the family are "replayed" in different life contexts on the unconscious level.

Every Company is a Family

Companies are also involved in this. Or to quote the psychologist Robert Betz: "Every company is a 'family', into which everyone unconsciously carries their family history and co-creates the state of the company and its success or failure" (Betz 2022). Companies are particularly suitable for reenacting learned behaviors and messages because they have clear parallels to family structures. They are hierarchically organized, their employees are in existential (economic) dependence and have a need for special protection and benevolent support, there are rivalries among colleagues, to name just a few parallels.

The Legacy of Childhood

It is primarily those experiences that we have made in our family of origin, with mother, father and siblings, and resulting learned behavior patterns, connections and beliefs, but also resources and positive developments, that steer us at the workplace along with our suppressed, rejected or also self-esteem-strengthening and confident feelings, influencing our behavior and attitudes.

Superiors are experienced more in the parental habitus. This is evident, for example, in employees who show themselves to superiors as particularly nice and adapted or also rebellious and uncomprehending. Superiors, on the other hand, may tend as a leader to behave like a strict or also benevolent father or a (too) understanding or strict mother. These are learned patterns from the role models of one's own childhood.

At the same time, many people know the feeling of powerlessness and deep shame when they find themselves unexpectedly and/or publicly criticized or attacked in a team meeting, for example. This concern ties in with negative experiences from childhood, where we were indeed helpless, small and helpless (Brandt et al. 2020).

> "I was on a quest with a client to find out why she becomes loud to the point of screaming in stressful situations. She herself experiences her behavior as embarrassing, but it seems unstoppable. It is an experience from her childhood. Her father 'wiped away' her perspectives for many years with the words: 'You have no idea, you are too small.' Becoming wise, having an idea, being able to analyze things, being faster than

others, are some of the wonderful qualities this woman has developed. But: Whenever this pain, this feeling of rejection and not being taken seriously, is triggered, this unwanted behavior shows itself."
Marianne Brandt, coach and organizational developer.

And here the circle closes: The family of origin not only offers the possibility of educational opportunities due to class or milieu affiliation, but also the development of self-esteem, ego strength, and thus psychological stability into old age. Positive and negative role models of the parent and grandparent generation, messages from childhood, unspoken things, frightening experiences, injustices, and positive ego reinforcement by important reference persons accompany us sustainably through life. They shape our attitudes, make us make decisions, control fear and trust—whether we are aware of it or not. The matrix of the family of origin lies hidden in our psyche as a basis for behavior and motivation.

Starting the examination of the regiment of role assignments with the origin of women means understanding what consciously and unconsciously drives women—where they give up power, believe they have none, and do not use it. Other factors such as a genetically determined personality type, a basic intellect or even circle of friends and place of residence determine in which nuances the mindset of women develops based on the family of origin. An existing basic intellect, coupled with a strong personality, allows women to become resilient despite hurdles due to their family constellation. Particularly conflict-ridden initial situations in childhood and adolescence spur some people on to further development. However, this increasingly distances them from their original family, which in turn can lead to conflicts between parents and child or to inner psychological conflicts and feelings of guilt, which intensify especially when parents become in need of care.

The Long Arm of Limitations
Whether and how the conditioning of daughters on the topic of success and career takes place also strongly depends on the family of origin. If parents' success-oriented thinking is limited on the basis of lack of education or class affiliation, this will directly influence the career thinking of daughters. The limitation concerns both achievable goals and the

2 Where Do We Come from and What Does that Do to Us?

definition of success. Parents from the lower middle class already see it as a success if their children graduate from high school. The maximum achievable goal from their point of view is then the high school diploma. Parents of daughters from the middle class set higher goals and expect an academic education. But the thinking rarely goes in the direction that points the way out of the regiment of role assignments: After the academic education follows a leadership job and then a board position. Or success is defined differently, namely as a combination of a secure job with a good income and enough time for hobbies and family. The thinking is already established in the parent generation in both cases, according to their respective experience and development level, and is passed on to the children. In other words: The children's thinking space is also initially limited and class-dependent.

For young women, this is one of the hurdles if they want to embark on career paths, because they consciously and unconsciously adopt the limitations of their parents. Expanding one's own thinking space means becoming aware of these limitations, actively striving for development, and if necessary, also going against resistance from the parent generation. Especially women who get much further in their careers than their parents are at risk of constantly having to justify this development. This particularly affects the daughter-mother relationship. This is often characterized by competition from the mothers. The glass ceiling that parents "install" long before employers is one of the biggest taboo topics. Women's development opponents are not only men, but also mothers, girlfriends, and colleagues.

> "Regardless of whether women admire their mothers or did not want to become or live like them at all, a very powerful glue of loyalty connects them. I often experience that women are successful and then—somehow—are stopped again. Often it is unconscious commands from the family systems that then take effect. The most shattering thing for me is when these women cannot even see what they are achieving, such as the run-down company that then also burns down, getting it back on its feet for free, using their own skills for the husband's business for free, taking care of three children and generating the main income for the family through clever rental of a property. This is taken for granted by this

woman. Do you think a man would act like this? No. The men I asked clearly say: *No*."

Marianne Brandt, coach and organizational developer.

The look back shows: Women in their own family of origin, but also in that of their later husband, had nothing to say. They were there, that's it. Therefore, when looking at role assignments and power relations, it is particularly about self-empowerment by the women themselves. That means, allowing oneself to strive for a powerful job based on acquired competencies and skills. And a job that is above the standard that the parent generation considered maximally achievable.

I dedicate the following chapters to the topic of functional and dysfunctional family constellations and describe using examples how these will affect daughters and their career path as well as their partnership. At the end of each chapter, I give recommendations, but still on a very factual level. The challenge is that the solutions seem right and logical, but are not so easy to implement in reality. Because the actual solution must take place on an emotional level.

In order for women to become powerful and assert themselves, it is essential that they confront their personal hurdles: their fears, their feelings of guilt, but also their loyalties and values. Because here lie the causes for unfulfilled equality, and that on the part of women. The inability to counteract aggression and dominant behavior from men, to offer little or nothing in return and to fall back into old role patterns, is related to fears and the fact that, for example in times of home office and homeschooling, women are left alone again with household and child. And this in turn is due to the sense of responsibility of working mothers, their shyness and fear of conflicts and confrontations with their partners.

> "A proven means: keeping women busy in power struggles. It distracts them from actively shaping and confidently and self-empoweredly using their opportunities. Instead, they too often get entangled in reactive mock battles."
>
> Dr. Ursula Koehler, systemic coach and expert for self-empowerment.

In conversations, women have repeatedly expressed to me the fear of being "abandoned". Women do almost everything to maintain a kind of family idyll for their children. If they do not stay in the confrontation, possibly supported by therapy or coaching, here begins the lie to themselves. Their own needs are denied.

A traditional relationship in the regiment of role assignments always involves two: a man and a woman, a boss and an employee, a *He* who dominates, and a *She* who lets herself be dominated. The resolution of this dilemma does not lie on the factual level, but in the emotional life of women. I will repeatedly address the emotions of women in the following chapters and show solutions here—knowing full well that this is the greatest challenge of this book, but also of the entire equality discussion. I am convinced: If women felt differently, we would not have this issue at all. And women feel the way they feel because there are role assignments by the family of origin and society, but also because they bring a different biological condition: they can have children.

Literature

Betz, Robert: „Jede Firma ist auch ein Kindergarten. Warum die inneren Kinder in Mitarbeiter und Führungskräften das Klima am Arbeitsplatz bestimmen und zerstören".https://robert-betz.com/fuer-unternehmen/jede-firma-ist-auch-ein-kindergarten/. Zugegriffen: 7. November 2022

Brandt, Marianne; Manthei, Doris; Lackner, Martina; Pamminger, Edith: Side-by-Side-Studie, 2020

3
The Power of Our Past and Origin

Abstract Functional or dysfunctional family systems of origin provide us with clues as to how the power of daughters can unfold later in their job or partnership. Women learn from the example of their mother and father. They adopt their assertiveness or adaptability and orient themselves according to the parental messages they receive. Mother and father can be positive or negative role models—depending on how they themselves live out relationships. Parents pass on their beliefs and values to the next generation, thereby influencing their thinking, actions, and behavior.

There are various family constellations and while reading, you may find the conditions from one constellation as well as from another constellation to be applicable to your own origin. A family remains an individual system. However, the following family types are intended to help you, even if they may seem categorical, to gain an impression of how your origin has affected your further life path and associated decisions. It is about their significance in relation to self-empowerment and the question of seizing power.

Based on the findings of the Side-by-Side study (Brandt et al. 2020), I show examples of how family systems of origin have affected the career path and partnerships of women. For each family constellation presented, I summarize learnings at the end of the section and provide recommendations for action and tips that are intended to help free oneself from the regiment of role assignments based on experiences in one's own parental home. Because those who understand where behavioral patterns, beliefs, and inclinations come from, know better where to start in order to change them for the sake of their own development.

> **Functional versus dysfunctional—the stories of Maria* and Verena***
>
> Maria* has never experienced affection. Her father is an alcoholic, becomes abusive when drunk, and tends to be violent. Her mother divorces when Maria is 15 years old. The mother is overwhelmed with the situation as a single parent. Maria increasingly distances herself from her at the beginning of puberty. Initially, she wants to stand by her side with advice, but soon realizes that her mother is falling into a deep hole and cannot be helped. Maria struggles through high school and starts studying. She works hard, first in her studies and later in her job. But she never knows if she is good enough and always feels on the verge of being overwhelmed. A leadership position would overwhelm Maria. She stays in the background, rather in the third row.
>
> Verena* is different: Both parents are working and lead a good marriage, characterized by mutual respect. And they also show this respect to Verena. They regard their daughter as a full member of the family from birth, albeit as someone who cannot yet clearly express her will, but clearly shows what she wants. Her parents take her wishes into account and support her in her plans. And so Verena knows very early on what she wants to do professionally. Her mother is a doctor and Verena's role model: She chooses medicine as her field of study. Verena struggles through medical school, but her mother is always by her side as a mentor. In her studies and later in her job, Verena has the certainty: There is a strong woman by my side and with my father in the background, nothing can happen to me—so let's go for the chief physician position! However, not to make her parents proud, but because there is an intrinsic motivation for it.
>
> *Name changed

Two families with different constellations—one functional, the other dysfunctional –, whose girls develop differently: Maria will probably keep herself afloat with temporary jobs or poorly paid academic jobs. She is likely to enter into a relationship with a man whom she thinks finally notices her—and will probably be disappointed (more on this in Chap. 5). On the other hand, Verena will determinedly go her own way because she has a supportive and benevolent parental home and also a role model: her mother.

What does psychology say about dysfunctional and functional family constellations? The following excerpts are from the Side-by-Side study (Brandt et al. 2020):

In dysfunctional families, boundaries are not or only conditionally allowed. Dysfunctional family members expect to be agreed with in everything. A "no" is not appropriate. Often, the constellations in the family are regulated by power-powerlessness relationships. This means, family members have to subordinate themselves to one person (or several people). Right and wrong lies in the power of definition of the dominant family members. These families have a high tension and conflict potential. The development of the children's self-esteem depends on the status that is granted to them in the family. With accusations and "you-are" messages, they are defined as a person, usually in the split between angel or scapegoat. Emotional affection is tied to conditions that are supposed to induce the children to certain behaviors (be good, bring honor, emotionally care for parents, etc.). In these systems, the children must develop special adaptation performance or resistances in order to exist in their families.

"I was never seen and recognized."
A participant of the Side-by-Side study from a dysfunctional family of origin.

Reading tip on the topic: https://www.selbsthilfehelden.com/dysfunktionale-familien-10-merkmale/

Functional families respect personal boundaries. Communication among each other is respectful, different opinions and needs are considered in decisions. The rules of living together are transparent and can also be changed. The children perceive themselves as lovable and independent personalities. There is a positive error culture in these families, so that the children neither develop sanction fears nor feel attacked in their personality when they make mistakes. Self-esteem is high. Trust in oneself as well as in others can develop well in these constellations, sometimes even to a certain naivety and an unconditional belief in the good in people.

> "My mother always emphasized that I should follow my own path."
> A participant of the Side-by-Side study from a functional family of origin.

Now delve deeper with me into the system of the family of origin. Learn to understand which constellations strongly influence your personal path in your job and in your partnership—perhaps because your mother never gave you the feeling of being powerful as a woman, or because your parents never allowed you self-empowerment, or because you grew up completely detached without any affirmation from your parents. These are different models that may have empowered you to strive for a good professional education—but then came a partner, a child, and the career slump. However, these factors did not just happen. Rather, you mostly chose them—consciously or unconsciously—or let happen what others definitely wanted. In other words: you let your life run its course and left the regiment to the role assignments.

3.1 Dysfunctional Family Constellations

3.1.1 Unrelated Parents

The story of Maria is about parents who were quite preoccupied with themselves: Her father has an addiction problem and her mother is overwhelmed, first in living together with an alcoholic, then as a single mother with a teenage daughter. The parents hardly relate to Maria, on the contrary: They burden their daughter with their own problems. They are unrelated.

Unrelated parents constantly revolve around themselves. Their own life and usually their own suffering are in the foreground. In such a detached family form, children cannot build stable relationships. Since their parents more or less ignore them in their personality, the uncertainty remains as to who they actually are.

In order to experience their own identity, children in these families tend to take on significant roles. They can take on a parental function. They feel responsible for the life and well-being of their parents. In systemic therapy, these cases are referred to as parentification.

There are also children who want to draw attention to themselves by achieving special performances and receiving awards. Being in competition and being successful in it means for them to be perceived positively by others.

For both forms of "making oneself noticeable", the children pay a high price. They quickly lose their childhood because they always have to function well or excellently. The respective demands can also be overwhelming, as they try to always do everything right. But since there is no real stop for these daughters—because it would have to be set by their parents—they run the risk of "overheating", i.e., mentally overburdening themselves. They are constantly in action or busy with top performances and hardly get any rest.

> "There's something wrong with my mother—she's not able to connect with people. I took over that for her."
> A participant of the Side-by-Side study with unrelated parents. Women from these family constellations are characterized by a high level of pragmatism. They take action, create structures, want to see results, are exceptionally quick in implementing tasks. Asking for support is rather difficult for these women. From a psychological point of view, this is very understandable, because they could only experience their right to exist in their family by achieving something on their own. Despite all the effort these women are willing to take on, their own self-image remains diffuse for them. They lack the perceptive gaze of their parents, which positively reflects their existence and also their right to exist (cf. Side-by-Side study, Brandt et al. 2020).

Theoretically, Maria has a disadvantage due to her unrelated parents, both in terms of her choice of partner and in striving for a leadership position. Since she has never learned, due to lack of feedback, that she is a valuable member of the family, and probably has never learned that she has competencies and strengths, Maria does not know how good and competent she actually is. And above all, how valuable she is. This leads to her presumably constantly selling herself short, because she cannot really assess herself. In addition, she constantly performs a lot in order to finally collect her reward. The probability is high that women like Maria choose partners who also do not see them, and find themselves in partnerships where they do more than they should—keyword household and child rearing. The same will happen on the professional level. Maria tends to let herself be exploited. She does not recommend herself for leadership positions because she does not know her worth. She is easily deterred from her chosen career because the slightest doubts from superiors about her competence shake her. She will probably end up in a dead end—either through starting a family or through burnout. Maria does not know her true power. She has no knowledge of what she is actually capable of. Therefore, she is subject to the regiment of role assignments, namely the role of a daughter of unrelated parents.

The unrelatedness of parents, of course, also has a consequence for sons. However, this deficit can be compensated by the male gender. It is not necessary for men to necessarily have a lot of knowledge about their own competencies, because the social system has in the past "flushed" them to where they wanted to go.

Women who come from such family constellations either do not reach leadership positions at all, because although they took on responsibility for their parents at a very early age, they were unable to build an adequate self-image and neither time nor resources were invested in their own development, or they give their life a right to exist through excessive performance. In the patriarchal structures of a company, this striving is then used for output, but not adequately rewarded, so that these women are rarely found in leadership positions. By the way, the same applies to private life: *She* runs the family business with household, child, and job, not *he*.

Women with unrelated parents have no idea what they are good at, as they grew up without feedback. Because they do not know how good they are, they usually stay with an employer who exploits them. Ambitious women must make the leap to a new job! They are also at risk of burnout. It arises not only from passion for the job, but also from the desire for recognition. Torn between the needs of the family and their own right to exist, these women face the end of their career before it has even begun.

The gap of ignorance becomes a power leak

The power of men is also based on the fact that women are insecure about their own abilities and competencies. This is advantageous for men: Equipped with greater self-confidence, they penetrate the gap of women's ignorance and "inflate themselves"—regardless of whether they are actually more competent than their female colleague.

Men quickly perceive women's doubts on a partly unconscious level and skillfully use them to oust potential competitors. These processes are becoming increasingly subtle. In the age of diversity and shortage of skilled workers, coupled with political pressure, many men feel threatened because they are aware that they are being asked to give up some of their power to women. This leads to further competitive thinking. As for openly dealing with conflicts with women, men also have to be increasingly careful due to improved protection against bullying and harassment. In private life, these competitions take place behind closed doors.

> **What needs to be done?**
> - Develop a realistic self-image. You need to become aware of what you can actually do! And what value you have for your partner and also for your employer. Coaches or therapists can support you in this process.
> - Those who know themselves well and are at peace with themselves are less dependent on the manipulative opinion of the other person and can take a powerful, emotionally independent position. Your weakening is not only based on ignorance, but also on the fact that this ignorance is used by the other person to weaken you. This creates a vicious circle that you can only escape if you start to recognize yourself.
> - Write down what you achieve and who benefits from this performance. If you find this difficult, ask a trusted person for support.

3.1.2 Dominant father and adapted mother

Maria's family history is not the only dysfunctional origin variant that can weaken women on their way to a career. Below I would like to introduce further forms that undermine the self-esteem and the power of design of women.

> **Sabine* and the burden of performance pressure**
>
> Sabine*, it seems, grew up in a well-off family. The father is a respected lawyer, the mother a doctor. With one difference: The self-employed father has the say in the family, also over the mother, who works part-time as a doctor in the hospital and enjoys her job. The patriarch is not even in agreement with the mother's few shift duties. He wants her to wait at home with dinner when he comes home late at night. The daughter experiences a constantly stressed mother who is torn between partner and job. After Sabine's birth, she stayed at home for years and took care of the child and household. The mother tries to submit to the father's wishes and considers giving up her job in the clinic again. Sabine, in turn, is under enormous pressure to perform: Her father expects excellent grades. Sabine studies law, although it does not correspond to her interests, because her father wants her to take over the law firm one day. She actually joins the law firm after her studies. Her dominant and domineering father does not act as a mentor, but increases his expectations of the daughter. Sabine considers leaving the law firm because she can no longer withstand the pressure.
> *Name changed

Sabine grew up in a dysfunctional family with a dominant father and a compliant mother. Dominant fathers see themselves as the breadwinners of the family and justify their authority in the family, to which everyone must submit. The mothers here tend to be more compliant and seem to have the same or a similar attitude as their husbands towards the children. They are usually not employed or their work is defined as insignificant. The upbringing is very strict, even to the point of using physical and psychological violence.

> "As a child, I was always afraid of sanctions. A hole in the tights was enough."

A participant in the Side-by-Side study with a dominant father.

The children in these families are judged by their performance, and they must meet their fathers' performance expectations. Competition among siblings is often further fueled. In adolescence, restrictions and prohibitions increase especially for the daughters, as they increasingly evade the father's control with increasing independence—this is equivalent to a family-internal taboo break. In these families, obedience and adaptation to the authority figure are particularly demanded from the women.

It is quite possible that these mothers encourage their daughters to become independent. However, a contradictory attitude is often evident here, as they derive their identity exclusively from their own motherhood and morally bind their daughters. Having missed their own life and denied feelings of competition towards their own daughter are usually the driving force for these and similar messages.

> "My mother said to me: Child, I want you to be happy—but your own freedom should not come at the expense of your children."
> A participant in the Side-by-Side study with a compliant mother.

The resulting inner conflict and low self-esteem is evident in the daughters, among other things, in that they choose partners who resemble their fathers or they easily let themselves be slowed down in their career ambitions. Their self-leadership shows clear breaks. A stop-and-go effect arises, so they constantly fluctuate between pursuing their own interests and satisfying the needs of their families (parents, husband, children) or, by proxy, their superiors (Brandt et al. 2020).

Sabine has never experienced women having power. She has no female role model. Her own mother cannot assert herself against the father. She did not become a woman with good self-esteem. From where? Suppressed by the father in her own needs, raised to obedience and not supported by the mother because she is too weak and has shaped her identity in motherhood. A self-confident daughter would have been hard for this mother to bear. Because she would have constantly shown her own deficit. The self-confidence could have developed over the course of her life, but it remains questionable to what extent.

Our parents encounter us again and again in life
If you grew up with a dominant father and a compliant mother, you can also find this constellation in the job, namely when you encounter a dominant boss. Now it shows whether your childhood behavior patterns repeat: Do you obediently adapt to your boss in the event of a conflict, like your mother to your father, or do you rebel against him, possibly to the point of breaking? What was your strategy in dealing with the dominant father in the past? And what do you do today? Or have you chosen a dominant, perhaps even violent, partner? Women reenact their father-daughter relationship by often choosing men who resemble their own fathers.

Possible behavior patterns
If you are still afraid of your unpredictable and violent father, consciously or unconsciously, it weakens you. Your assertiveness is blocked. For your behavior this means: You like to take cover, tend to justify yourself when criticized, remain simply "invisible" or suffer silently—always in the tension between your own needs and adaptation. These are some of the possible behavior patterns with which you encounter situations and people who trigger your early experienced violence scenarios. The conscious confrontation with the topic helps to recognize them.

Some women with these childhood experiences tend to adapt as followers in a patriarchal system or to use the advantages of being a follower for themselves, because they take the path of least resistance, to name just a few effects. The dilemma: These women maintain a violent system. In this victim attitude—and of course they take it when they are dominated—they only very hesitantly manage to break away from a violent relationship or an unfavorable boss-employee constellation. Their fear of the power of the father/boss binds them. With this behavior, they unconsciously strengthen the power of the dominant counterpart and thus even favor the violence spiral—and do not find the way out of the regime of role attributions.

What needs to be done?
- You cannot break patterns of violence from your childhood without professional support. If you want to advance in your job and your other relationships, you need to work on yourself. It is best to seek psychological-therapeutic help or coaching for this. This is not a sign of weakness, but of strength! As long as you unconsciously see yourself as a victim because your self-image shows a high victim identification, you will not gain power. I am talking here in the first step about self-empowerment: You switch from victim status to "doer status" by leaving situations and people who trigger your early experienced violence scenarios and associated fears, or by learning strategies on how to powerfully confront your violent counterpart. The same principle also applies to a partnership with a dominant violent man.
- Dealing with such people can indeed be trained, but whether such a relationship is good for you is questionable. Dominant men with high aggression potential usually do not change. Often, the only solution is to detach from these bonds.

3.1.3 Dominant Mother and Self-Insecure Father

In this constellation, the mothers appear to be the head of the family. That is, they are the main breadwinners and reliable reference persons for their children. The fathers do not have a steady job, appear rather self-insecure, and often come from dominant family systems where they have not met their parents' expectations.

Helga* and the Unreliable Father

Helga* grows up with a father who keeps disappearing. He makes no decisions, leaving the earning of the family income, household, and children to his wife. He himself gets by with odd jobs or relies on social assistance. He spends the money on cigarettes and alcohol. Helga's mother knows that everything depends on her. She earns the family's living with numerous cleaning jobs and is afraid of losing them and "sinking" in life. She cannot rely on her husband, and she takes care of her two children as best she can. Between two cleaning jobs, she cooks lunch when the children come home from school. The children are then left to their own devices for homework, as the father does not take on a supportive role and the mother is not available due to her work commitments—and can increasingly less follow the tasks of the children.
   *Name changed

Codependent Couple Constellations

In the mentioned example, it is a codependent couple constellation. Family secrets remain hidden here, the children often know nothing about serious problems, such as addiction problems of a parent. Nevertheless, they subtly affect the families. For the children, the feeling that something is "not right" can be very burdensome. They develop a distrust of their parents or one parent over many years and cannot explain why this is so. They perceive that their parents' marriage is broken, and yet these almost desperately stay together. The children's wishes for separation are put off or ignored.

> "My mother did not want to separate from our father, even though I asked her to do so again and again."
> A participant of the Side-by-Side study with codependent parents.

Both parents equally cling to the relationship, even if they have to accept high psychological burdens for all family members. In psychology, it is assumed that in this couple constellation, both parents struggle with existential fears, namely not being able to cope with life alone.

These childhood experiences lead to special autonomy efforts in adulthood. Trusting others and waiting for promises to be fulfilled is something children from such constellations have not experienced in their childhood and adolescence.

> "I never want to become dependent on anyone. I want to do my own thing."
> A participant of the Side-by-Side study with codependent parents.

As adults, they therefore prefer to—sometimes prematurely and activistically—"get things done". In psychology, this approach is understood as a solution mechanism to escape their own feeling of powerlessness, which is reflected in their parents (Source: Side-by-Side study, Brandt et al. 2020).

Helga experiences a mother who is fearful in life, even though she is the main breadwinner of the family. Neither the father nor the mother can be relied upon. Instead, Helga experiences that both are powerless and tries to compensate for this. She gets into relationship constellations where both are afraid—herself, her partner, or an insecure boss. The underlying message here is: power and fear are mutually exclusive.

Perhaps you also grew up this way? Your mother alone determined and organized the family's everyday life, and your insecure father played the "strong Max" for appearances? Then this relationship may be repeating itself in your personal work relationship or your partnership, namely when you have a weak superior and as an assistant or team leader you are actually the secret boss of the whole department. But why don't you officially run the show as the boss, but operate from the shadows?

Mutual Dependence Repeats Itself in the Job
Let's take another look at Helga's parents: Both were dependent on each other—the father needed the mother to function, and the mother needed him to maintain the status of a wife and to somewhat bask in the feeling of emotional security, which, however, resembled a false sense of security. This mutual dependence repeats itself everywhere. Men need women to keep things running. Women need the job to secure their livelihood, and "enjoy" the secret power, because they usually operate from the second row. The roles are clearly distributed: The boss knows that women are better, they are more qualified, work more stringently and efficiently, especially when they are mothers, and use their skills and competence for the benefit of the company, as long as they do not dispute his position. And she knows that she has secret power and her livelihood as long as she submits to the subordinate role. She knows about her power, without having to bear the responsibility for it, because responsibility scares her.

> As hierarchically subordinate "shadow-powerful", you will always remain in the shadow of your superior, even though you achieve a lot and your skills would be suitable for the official leadership role. What you actually do is not financially rewarded. You belittle yourself. Are you aware of this? The fact is: In this way, you prevent your own career!

Secret power is a form of power that can only take place in the second row—professionally in subordinate positions or privately, by the woman having the say in family life with husband and/or children, without being the main provider. However, women only benefit emotionally from this power because it is limited to the relationship level. They do not earn much money with this apparent power, nor can they exert influence in public space.

> **Example**
>
> "A case study from psychological practice: She studies psychology, he medicine. During their studies, the first child is born. Both complete their studies. Two more children follow. The mother decides not to work as a psychologist, but takes care of the offspring, house and garden alone and works as an assistant in her husband's general practice. She is the emotional boss at home, but financially completely dependent on her husband. And the marriage is not going well. In the event of a divorce, she would lose her status as a doctor's wife and slide into old-age poverty."
>
> Edith Pamminger, clinical and health psychologist, systemic psychotherapist.

> **What to do?**
>
> - Ask yourself: Are you afraid of taking responsibility and stepping out of the shadow? Do you even think that you do not have the right to want more than the regiment of role assignments allows you? Are you satisfied with the secret power and the little recognition that comes out for you, while your boss reaps the fruits of your work with corresponding payment?
> - Decide: Do you want to continue acting as a secret boss with apparent power, or do you finally try to sit in the boss's chair yourself and transform your skills into real power? At this point, I would also like to emphasize that not all women have to strive for leadership positions, because there are simply too few of these positions. The question is rather: What would be an honest way of dealing with one's own power aspirations?

3.1.4 Competing Parents

In this constellation, both parents or one parent are in competition with their own daughters. Competitions between mothers and daughters are more well-known. However, this phenomenon also exists in relation to daughters and fathers.

> **Hanna* and her mother's expectations**
>
> Hanna* is limited by her mother. She tirelessly tries to get Hanna on the track she deems right. Right, from the mother's point of view, is a course of study that will later allow family and career to be easily combined. She wants Hanna to become a teacher, just like herself. But Hanna wants to study medicine. Hanna dreams of a big career as a surgeon, preferably with her own practice. The mother, on the other hand, thinks of a career as a high school teacher, in the same small town, close to the daycare and elementary school and of course close to the mother. After all, she wants to continue participating in Hanna's life and see the grandchildren grow up. But Hanna's dream does not (yet) include children. The expectations are far apart.
> *Name changed

Hanna has a mother who competes with her, she has a competing mother. The following explanations about competing parents are taken from the Side-by-Side study (Brandt et al. 2020):

Competitive mothers want their daughters not to develop their own life plan, but to follow in their footsteps. They try to impose their own life concept on their daughters. Performance-oriented mothers, for example, expect the same performance habitus. Mothers who have sacrificed themselves for the family expect the same self-sacrifice they have made from their daughters. These daughters run the risk of never being able to meet their mothers' expectations, even as adult women. Competitive mothers perceive their own life concept as the optimal one. This is at least true for the external representation, behind the facade there is a lot of frustration—and the realization that their own life has not really gone well. If the daughters then decide on a completely different path and this path also works well, it is hard for these mothers to bear.

> "My mother hated me at times because I was different from her."
> A participant in the Side-by-Side study with a competitive mother.

Competitive feelings of fathers towards their daughters are the opposite. Insecure fathers, who have little to show professionally or who play with the image of refusing a career, undermine their daughters in their developmental desires. Higher education is rejected as unnecessary, the circle of friends of the daughters with similar ambitions is disparaged. These fathers want to decide on their daughters' career choices and bind them in dependencies—if necessary, they use fear: Studying is the direct path to unemployment. Every step towards their daughters' own autonomy is understood as a threat and criticism of life. Therefore, it is so important that the daughters function in the sense of the fathers.

> "My sister and I are both emancipated. We live a completely different life, which intimidates our father."
> A participant in the Side-by-Side study with a competitive father.

Daughters of competitive parents are characterized by a very high willingness to perform and career ambition. Developing personally and forming their own identity is of great importance to these women. On the unconscious level, the motive of having achieved the maximum as an independent personality against resistance and appropriating messages from the parents is effective. However, their self-esteem is fragile due to the aggressive rejection of their parents and the confidence in their own competencies is weakened. They always have a feeling of not being enough, no matter what they achieve and accomplish.

In the case of Hanna, her ambition for power is constantly limited—either by the competitive mother or by the insecure father. Hanna not only wants to fulfill a dream, she also dreams a dream that is far beyond the professional possibilities of the mother, both financially and in terms of image and status. The daughter will far surpass her mother and leave the milieu she comes from.

This scares the mother, primarily because with top career prospects it is not clear whether her daughter will have children and possibly a future life content of the mother will be omitted. In the background and much more serious, Hanna's striving means: The daughter shows the mother how much a woman can achieve. She holds up a mirror to her—and probably touches old longings of her mother, which she could not realize in her time. And so the mother tries her "best" to dissuade Hanna from her dream.

While patriarchal, insecure fathers cannot bear competent daughters, it is also mothers who put obstacles in the daughters' way. When mothers say: "My children should have it better", this is often not true. Because when daughters are more educated than they are through a higher school degree and consequently step out of the parental value system and leave their milieu, this is usually hard for mothers to bear. With what the daughter does, she holds up a mirror to her mother, which shows a painful picture: You did not achieve this yourself. You did not have these rights. You did not take your chances.

The Effect of Deeper Truths
This reflection is repeated in companies: Competent and well-educated young women are a threat to male and female executives. Because they fuel their fear of competition. When these young women meet patriarchal or dominant superiors, or female superiors who had to work hard for their top position and have therefore become hard, then these, out of their own experienced humiliation, coupled with the fear of competition, make life difficult for these young women, instead of welcoming and promoting them.

Some women lack the sharp eye for the deeper truths. They do not see through the game of mothers, fathers, and superiors, but take it as true that, for example, lack of competence does not lead to a leadership position, and then look for the blame in themselves!

They must assume that the competitive, sometimes aggressive behavior of some men and women will not change even in times of skilled labor shortage and women's promotion. Behaviors that have developed and manifested over thousands of years cannot be changed by a quota or diversity efforts within a few years. Because these are deeply seated emotions: the fear for one's own job, the humiliation one has experienced, the efforts that men also have to make to get to the top, etc. Whether in small talk in the tea kitchen, in a one-on-one conversation or in a meeting—you will encounter this behavior again and again.

> Being attacked means that someone wants to degrade you to a victim, but whether *he* or *she* wins this game, you have partly in your own hands. Make it clear to yourself: Power has the one who appears powerful.

> **What to do?**
> - Ask yourself: How do I recognize that I am not the problem, but rather my superior's fear of me?
> - Relativize the power of your "opponent": Actively defend against attacks and counter them. Ducking or making yourself invisible signals to your counterpart that you are avoiding confrontation or accepting the victim role.
> - Train your communication and your appearance! Prepare sentences that you have ready when you are verbally attacked: How do I react when the boss puts me down, even though he knows I was good? What do I say when I am verbally abused? Practice quick-wittedness. And pay attention to your body language. If necessary, seek professional help.

3.1.5 Insecure and Fearful Parents

Fearful parents often lacked secure attachments in childhood or they grew up in rigid, violent situations that made them extremely frightened. A high need for security and protection is strongly pronounced in these parents, not only in childhood, but also as adolescents and adults. Their own career choice and professional activity are decided according to solid criteria, not according to desire or inclinations. Such highly adapted and self-uncertain parents instill the following message in their children: "Life is dangerous, but we don't know when and how." Regardless of whether the parents or the whole family had to go through existential crises in the course of life, the message remains set and shapes their children sustainably. In puberty, these children also do not experience strengthening and encouragement to dare something new or to actively approach life (Source: Side-by-Side Study, Brandt et al. 2020).

> **Daniela* and her parents' fear**
>
> Daniela* spends her childhood in the former GDR. When the change comes, her parents seize the opportunity to move to West Berlin. The father soon has a job as an engineer, the mother, an administrative employee, searches for a long time for a job. Both find the new life difficult. The mother in particular suffers from being on her own and having to organize her life herself. Although the GDR had major disadvantages, she could rely on being taken care of here. She can hardly fit into the new system of the Federal Republic. The fear she brought from her homeland, and the fear of not making it in the new homeland, burden her so much that she develops depression. The father is busy with his own fears and cannot support the mother. He occasionally sinks into melancholy.
>   *Name changed

Daniela grows up with insecure, fearful parents. She does not experience that people generally have power or can seize power. In her childhood, she grew up in an autocratic system and in freedom her parents could not do anything with the gained freedom. On the contrary: Freedom became a psychological threat. And the chance for power in the sense of self-empowerment towards a more fulfilling life could not be seized by both parents. This background of experience is missing for Daniela. She herself will hardly be able to seize power from within. In systemic therapy, we speak of a fear transmission often traumatized mothers to their daughters. The self-esteem of these daughters is little developed by these experiences and the confidence in their own leadership is broken.

> "My parents had good, secure jobs in the GDR. After the change, both were very afraid of not making it. My mother overdid it. That made her mentally ill. That still has an effect today."
> Daniela (name changed), participant in the Side-by-Side study.

A childhood with fearful parents is a major career killer. Women's confidence in themselves is not developed. They classify life as dangerous. If they have children, life becomes even "more dangerous" for them because more uncertainties are added. Therefore, they strive for secure jobs. Since jobs in the private sector or self-employment are associated with more risks, they tend to positions in the public service. But here the remuneration and the chance for further development are lower.

Those who are afraid seek protection. Also in the form of a secure job. Fearful people—whether men or women—therefore orient themselves towards jobs that offer security. For women, the need for security is even greater with a view to motherhood.

Even though the shortage of skilled workers opens up many opportunities for well-educated women, they have to struggle with career obstacles that particularly stand in the way of women from this family constellation: Every new job harbors unknowns and fuels uncertainties. If a change of location is necessary for the job, it becomes difficult. Moving with children and a husband with a well-paid job becomes a major challenge here. As a rule, these women follow their husbands, not the other way around.

> **What to do?**
> - Work on your fear patterns! Be aware: Due to stress at work, bullying in everyday work or challenges such as a pandemic, fears can become anxiety disorders. If these remain untreated, this can lead to incapacity to work.
> - Look at your relationship! Your fearfulness also has an effect at the couple level. You also strive for security here—and thus not for power or equality. You will strive for the relationship to offer you security. Fearful women do not negotiate, neither for equal distribution of household and childcare nor for other aspects of an equal relationship. In constant fear that the relationship could break up, they put up with a lot.

3.2 Functional Family Constellations

Parents as Positive Role Models
Remember the story of Verena at the beginning of the chapter. Verena comes from a family where the parents serve as positive role models. In systemic therapy, this is referred to as a functional family constellation, the optimal case. The following explanations are taken from the Side-by-Side study (Brandt et al. 2020):

Daughters from functional family constellations describe their mothers as strong and proactive, and their fathers as unconventional and attentive. The parents' relationship was balanced and on an equal footing. Role stereotypes did not exist or did not play a role in the parents' internal relationship. In some cases, even their grandparents set this example by throwing conventional norms overboard and instead encouraging their children to stand up for themselves.

> "My parents have reinvented themselves a hundred times."
> A participant of the Side-by-Side study with parents as positive role models.

Crises and changes, which occur repeatedly in families, are actively and constructively addressed by parents in this constellation. The assurance that there are always solutions to all the problems that life presents is not only conveyed but also lived out. The parents are positive role models for their children, who continue to strengthen them as adults today. The professional achievements of their mothers play a significant role in the daughters' career paths.

> "My mother was my role model—from a cleaner to a secretary."
> A participant of the Side-by-Side study with parents as positive role models.

Daughters from this constellation can experiment with what interests them from an early age. The parents are proud of their daughters and positively encourage them to take control of their own lives.

The daughters' self-esteem and identity formation during puberty is supported by their parents through high emotional security. Even when something doesn't work out, the fact that they tried is positively connoted.

Women from these families are characterized by a great trust in their own ability to act and that of others. They live with the understanding that every person is entitled to their own development and identity, in mutually supportive partnerships.

> "Try it out. If it doesn't work, you can come back."
> A participant of the Side-by-Side study with parents as positive role models.

Verena comes from a family that is well established in life, the relationships among each other are characterized by respect. Verena learns very early that she is a valuable person. Misbehavior does not result in negative consequences. Her self-esteem is good and Verena was able to develop a strong sense of self. These are very good prerequisites for reaching positions of power. Power does not scare Verena—and if she has the motivation for it, she will strive for powerful positions.

In conclusion, it can be stated that few women come from functional family constellations. Because the parent generation, who had children in the 1960s, was characterized by a strongly patriarchal society that existed hierarchically or through violence. In other words: Most mothers and fathers were not positive role models for today's women over 50. Women born in the 1970s and 1980s know from their mothers the idea of wanting more, but the conviction is fragile, as the mothers served more as a deterrent. They were usually housewives or only marginally employed and had few rights. Women born around the millennium already know the price of success from their mothers, who had to work hard for it. Therefore, for many young women, a career or top career is only tempting to a certain extent. It is not due to a lack of competencies and qualifications or a deficiency in their leadership skills: Young women no longer want to submit to the system of obedience and adaptation in companies. Some women therefore choose the path of self-employment, part-time, if they are mothers. However, they often cannot live on this income. They remain financially dependent on the man.

Women of this age only recommend themselves for a top leadership position to a limited extent, because they often lack the desire and the will to power. Pursuing a career with 60 working hours or more, perhaps even with a child, is not desirable for these women. And probably not for men either. What is missing here is a good and healthy balance between work and leisure.

No Career, but …

Every woman who rejects a professional development for herself still pays a price. Namely, the price of lifelong dependence—either on the man as a lifelong full provider or on the parents. Where parents or grandparents have previously "worked hard", wealth has grown. The inheritance ensures that today's daughters do not go completely penniless into retirement, at least in certain layers. But that means: Those who expect an inheritance do not have to work as hard as others, but are therefore morally obliged—to lifelong attention, to the care and support of those who have provided for the inheritance. This creates a binding dilemma characterized by dependencies.

"A financial dependency could perhaps be resolved quite quickly, but often a well-disguised emotional dependency or insecurity lurks behind it. If it remains undetected and unresolved, the parties involved subconsciously sabotage themselves over and over again to stay in this familiar pattern."
Dr. Ursula Koehler, systemic coach and expert for self-empowerment.

> Those who are dependent will never be powerful. Especially powerful people, who are prone to abuse of power, make people dependent in order to secure their own power. Women who put themselves in emotional or financial dependence, therefore, give up a certain amount of desires and needs as well as control over their own lives.

> **What should be done?**
> - Become aware early on of the personal consequences of your life decisions!
> - Make it clear to yourself who becomes dependent for what reasons and carefully weigh up what "price" you are willing to pay. Your own career can then appear in a new light. Power begins for you where you are neither financially nor emotionally dependent.

Literature

Brandt, Marianne; Manthei, Doris; Lackner, Martina; Pamminger, Edith: Side by Side-Studie, 2020

4

When Hormones Take the Lead

Abstract The hormonal development that young girls undergo during puberty leads them to be overly guided by their emotions in their upcoming partner selection. This means that they choose men based on criteria relevant to reproduction. In the search for a suitable partner, the focus is not on compatibility with their own career ambitions.

We have extensively dealt with theories on the development of self-esteem and ego strength. In the following chapters, I would like to focus on the emotions of women—they are something like the icing on the cake against the backdrop of factors already presented. Emotions cement experiences that women have. They illuminate and evaluate crucial life situations and people from an emotional perspective and then derive behaviors from them—for dealing with partners, colleagues, bosses, and their own offspring.

As a psychologist, I primarily focus on the intrapsychic and external psychological factors regarding the power development of women. Nevertheless, I allow myself to provide insights into the hormonal development of both sexes and what can be derived from it.

Testosterone as a driving force
In the phase of sexual maturity, the sexes "separate" in the formation of a different body structure and sexual characteristics, but also in terms of behaviors and levels of meaning. This happens under the influence of a different hormonal development: While estrogen predominates in women after going through this developmental phase, the testosterone level in men's blood is higher and even multiple times higher, as evolutionary biologist Carole Hooven (Hooven 2021) describes. Hooven found in her studies that testosterone is a driving force in conditioning men for competition, increasing their propensity for violence, their hunger for status and for sexual partners. Even though we are humans and can reflect on our own behavior, we still resemble animals as a product of millions of years of evolution. The hormone testosterone, in combination with genes and culture, shapes men and controls their aggressive behavior. However, this theory does not provide a sufficient explanation for the emergence of patriarchally dominated forms of society. Since the testosterone level in women is significantly lower, it can be concluded that women behave more adaptively, their level of aggression and propensity for violence are significantly lower. This influences how they live partnerships or how and with what means they pursue or enforce career paths. I will go into this in more detail later.

Role Models 2.0
In addition, with the formation of female sexual organs, a woman's body is conditioned for reproduction. Puberty lays the foundations for the continuation of humanity. The behavior of young girls is initially aimed at finding role models. No, they are not managers or politicians that girls today look up to. They are influencers and protagonists of the glamour world, showing them how they should look: slim, made up, in the right clothing look, with appropriate poses and pouting lips. Not to convince a company of themselves in a job interview, no—for some girls, this is about upgrading their own person to eventually attract a male counterpart for mating. Insecure adolescents, in this case girls, seek support and orientation in social networks. Here they seek answers to the question: What do I have to do as a girl to be trendy, to be liked by others, to get attention, in short: to get a value?

The insignificance of motherhood
The underlying motive in the search for orientation and identification is to build an identity as a future woman in order to reproduce and then ensure the survival of the offspring before one passes away. In between, humanity is busy securing its own life. The original biological "mission" is overlaid by a cultural development that no longer pays real attention to motherhood. In my view, this is one of the reasons why mothers are even lower in the social hierarchy than women—the act of conception, pregnancy, and upbringing is seen as redundant in an affluent society. No importance is attributed to a mother—unless it comes to the discussion about pensions and the shortage of skilled workers.

Suitable gene pool more important than suitable mindset
Young women, driven by hormones and millions of years old "programs", look for men with whom they can reproduce—but not men who support them in their professional development. The search for a suitable gene pool is more important than the search for a suitable mindset for their own career aspirations. The topic of partnership and career development for women already becomes important when it comes to choosing a profession. A choice that must be family-compatible—especially when it turns out that the partner has a different idea of life together or sticks to certain role assignments. Although studies show that women are better educated and have better degrees, a different film is running subliminally. And this film begins with the conscious or unconscious search for a suitable man.

The power of the myth disempowers self-efficacy
In the decision for a partner and the subsequent founding of a family, many women lose power over their own lives. All that they have acquired in terms of self-esteem, competence, and qualification becomes fragile at this point. They give in, especially on an emotional level. This is where the image of the prince on the white horse, leading them to the wedding altar as the crowning glory of their lives, is created. This image is then surpassed by the myth of the completeness of a family, which is only established through children. Here we move in the emotional space of women. These ideas give women security and a sense of

well-being, a kind of state of happiness that gives their life meaning. This myth is maintained—through fairy tales, stories, books, social media, societal values, the family environment, and through a certain hormonal state that occurs in the phase of falling in love or later at the birth of a child. In many women, hormones now take the lead and largely determine the emotional life of women.

Glorification Ensures Continuity
What sounds like a shortcoming of women actually ensures the existence of humanity. If young women were to view partnership and motherhood from a ruthlessly realistic perspective and not succumb to the glorification of this state, the desire for reproduction would only remain in a few women. Glorification is a necessary prerequisite for humanity to continue to reproduce.

Even if it may sound like women are subject to their hormonal fluctuations, it should be noted: they are not. Women just need to be aware that a different cocktail of hormones influences their behaviors—and develop alternative strategies for this.

> Just because I know that love can blind, because during the phase of infatuation there is indeed a lack of critical view of the partner, I do not have to surrender to this feeling. I can make a completely realistic assessment of my partner at any time—if I want to.

> "Perhaps it would be useful to make boys and girls aware of their roles, possible life plans, and their pitfalls in school subjects such as ethics or social learning. To talk with girls (!) about the consequences of part-time work, financial dependence, and consequences for retirement and to bring the pitfalls into the consciousness of boys and girls. To engage in concrete discussions with young people about traditional roles and role changes and to look for changes and new solutions that also empower girls."
> Edith Pamminger, clinical and health psychologist, systemic psychotherapist.

Literature

Hooven, Carole: "T: The Story of Testosterone, the Hormone That Dominates and Divides Us.", Henry Holt 2021

5

The Balancing Act between Partnership, Motherhood, and Career

Abstract The choice of partner and the importance women attach to their motherhood are not only career killers or career boosters, but are also directly related to the development of their self-esteem and how women thereby entangle themselves in role assignments and get stuck in them. Behind this are deep-seated feelings of guilt, fear, and shame that strictly regulate the women: The role assigned to them must be fulfilled, from the compliant partner to the supermother. Any deviation from the role could, in their view, lead to a negative consequence.

In my perception, women lose themselves in their needs, goals, and dreams—initially when they enter a partnership, but even more so when they become mothers and also have career ambitions. They are torn between various demands, expectations, and everyday necessities. They exhaust themselves on an organizational level to manage household and child-rearing alongside their job, and even more so on an emotional level, where feelings of guilt, fear of failure, and the fear of not meeting the expectations of their environment tug at them. And so, women often adapt to a predetermined role because it means less struggle and friction. The solution lies in the right choice of partner, a critical view of the private environment regarding support and loyalty, and in beneficial negotiations with the partner and other potential supporters for the compatibility of family and career. One thing is particularly important for women: not to give negative burdensome emotions the power over decisions. Because these emotions, which arise from role conflicts, lead to wrong strategies and behaviors that burn out women.

Equal treatment starts with each woman herself

I want to break with a narrative: namely that equal treatment would only be a task for men or companies. When women deal with the topic of partnership, motherhood, and career, they sooner or later end up with the issue of "incompatibility of job and family". And with that, we inevitably end up with the demand for mother- and father-friendly workplaces. This has consequences. Because on a private level this means: We direct the demand for participation in household and child-rearing to men or turn to politics with the demand for laws that enable women to reach leadership positions. Specifically, this means: One side is asked to create suitable conditions so that women can combine family life and career. Who is left out in these discussions are the women themselves! Therefore, my narrative is: If a woman demands equal treatment from men, she must first put herself in a mental and emotional position that presupposes equality.

> "I can only support this new narrative! To make progress here, all screws must be turned, including ourselves."
> Dr. Angelika-Weinländer-Mölders, chemist, manager, and co-editor of *Side by Side—Men at the side of successful women*

Therefore, please ask yourself the following:

- Do you see yourself as valuable?
- As valuable as your husband?
- Do you put yourself on a par with your superior in terms of human value?
- Do you discuss with men in a way that leaves no doubt that you can make a valuable contribution?

5 The Balancing Act between Partnership, Motherhood, and Career

- Do you naturally deal with your partner and boss on an equal footing?
- Are you aware that you have the same rights as your male counterpart, or do you always see yourself one step below?
- Do you look up to men?
- Are you in begging mode?
- Or do you think the other person knows better and has better performance to show?
- Do you believe you are not good enough or have not tried hard enough?

If all these questions, which I have directed at you, are part of your self-image and have thus become a persistent but continuous companion in everyday life, then your demand for equal treatment is a hollow affair that will probably not really occur in your life.

Why not? Well, if you do not see yourself as valuable and do not put yourself on a par with men, why should men then treat you as a valuable person if you cannot do it yourself? Many women talk about their partner or boss on this topic, but they mean themselves. One of the causes is that women do not see themselves as equal based on learned role models. In short: They do not allow themselves equality. Because any deviation from the learned and assigned role leads to feelings of guilt and a bad conscience. The belief then seems to be: "I as a woman do not fulfill my role or not correctly."

> Placing yourself "under" the man results in him not believing your demand for equality. He will not take you seriously and will laugh at you. In this way, you cement the image of women, that men can "soften" women, keep them small, belittle them, etc. A vicious circle: The less you value yourself, the less a man will value you.

"There are several structural traps in the regiment of role assignments: Family work is free as long as it is provided by the partner. It starts to cost something when a nanny, day mother, and household help come in or the child goes to daycare. Put it to the test. How many hours do you spend a week on family work? The minimum wage is twelve euros. You won't make it with 20 hours. Let's assume 30 or 40 hours because you are well organized—so 360 or 480 euros gross per week. It is the time that helps your husband to make a career and allows him to increase the classic 40-hour week to 60 hours. He earns more, you are dependent on his income, even if you are an economic community. You can't make up for this time in terms of salary and career."

Marianne Brandt, coach and organizational developer.

New Models are Needed

As already explained, women often lack the development of self-esteem and ego strength, often from childhood. Experiences of violence in the family of origin can cause a woman to experience herself as not or little valuable. Her perceived worthlessness or doubts about it have their origin here. And they lead to a disastrous mixture with the choice of partner, motherhood, and later with professional advancement, which makes the tension triangle of partnership—child—career a ticking time bomb for women's role understanding. Young women lose their power in this tension triangle, which they have (painfully) worked for up to this point.

I would like to give you a guide at this point on how to get out of the perceived worthlessness and inequality. But I find this topic too complex to show suitable solutions for every woman in a book. Books cannot compensate for the perceived deficit with well-formulated and intelligent-sounding sentences and descriptions, let alone guide a change. I can only give impulses for this. It requires a therapeutic process to work through injuries, traumas, wounds, or other circumstances that have led to the described mental condition. These are often lengthy processes. If you feel affected, I wish you to go this way with a therapist. Take your times of reflection to recognize connections, develop alternative action or thought patterns, and deal with your own emotions. Guides offer intellectual food, but are not suitable to remedy an actual deficiency, such as low self-esteem.

What you always need, however, is the unconditional will to step out of an apparent comfort zone, out of a non-appreciative situation, out of bad conditions. Because one thing is certain: the perceived inequality, even if it hurts, becomes a "beloved" companion over the years.

After all, stepping out of a role assignment can also mean the end of a marriage or job loss. Through emotional and financial dependencies, women become blackmailable. Above self-confident women who want to avoid dependencies and meet men at eye level, there is always a sword of Damocles. Women must be aware of this.

> Remember: Power in its negative form always seeks someone who can be dominated.

5.1 Power at First Sight?

What happens when two people get to know and love each other? In short: Either the spark jumps right away and the tingling in the stomach becomes more and more intense or you find each other nice and at some point the spark jumps. But very complex processes take place within the psyche. Did you know that women choose partners who resemble their fathers? Certain behaviors, certain patterns and values, body language, smell or appearance, which remind of the first male reference person in a woman's life, are triggers for daughters. They fall in love, so to speak, again in their father, 2.0.

This can be good if women were treated respectfully by their own father. They will look for a partner who also lives this value: a partner at eye level. The first male reference person in their life has raised them with respect and appreciation. However, those who grew up in structures of violence run into the next spiral of violence. These daughters are far from eye level. One would think that women learn from their history and distance themselves from such men. But the exact opposite is the case. As already mentioned, people constantly try to re-enact their own life story or the role they have taken here. Violence—physical, emotional or verbal—is familiar to them, even if they have suffered from it. It is the only form of affection they know. So they look for what is familiar to them. The father still has power over them—even when they have long since detached themselves from the family of origin.

Men, on the other hand, are driven differently in their search for a partner: Their testosterone switches to hunting instinct. The male hormone constantly fuels the search for a suitable sexual partner and a woman who will pamper him—just like his own mother. At this point, it becomes clear what role women will take from a man's perspective.

In the interaction of the two sexes, the question of power enters the playing field: Who will prevail when it comes to childcare, career ambitions or household management?

The power question, usually clearly defined by the man, is strongly dependent on the type of man, which I will go into in more detail in Sect. 5.2.

> Note: What types of men can you as a woman encounter?

5.2 Partnerships—from Career Supporters to Career Brakes

Women want partners at their side who act on an equal footing with them and wish for development opportunities for both. This is an ideal that sometimes seems to work, sometimes not. I will introduce you to several models of how men want to live a relationship in 2023.

5.2.1 The Classic: Side by Side with the "Yes-but" Man

A widespread model is the relationship with the "yes-but" man, a pseudo-ideal case and a classic in couple relationships, whose attitude can be summed up with "Honey, you can certainly make a career, but …". The closer examination of this model is taken from the Side-by-Side study (Brandt et al. 2020):

At first glance, some aspects of these relationships may seem like an ideal couple's life. The differences only become apparent when certain, usually unspoken, rules are violated. There are different degrees of this:

5 The Balancing Act between Partnership, Motherhood, and Career

The "but" can refer to specific areas. It can sometimes be a loud or a quiet "but". Messages that women hear from their men can include:

- Career yes, but without personal restrictions for me.
- Career yes, but I still want to be taken care of.
- Career yes, but not with overtime.
- Career yes, but don't earn more money than me.
- Career yes, but please don't forget our children.

> "As long as I don't work too many hours, it's fine."
> A participant of the Side-by-Side study 2020.

Some women are part of the problem of lack of equality. They raise their sons to be little princes who don't have to take on tasks in the household or in other areas outside of work. Such sons look for a partner who serves as Mom 2.0, but—unlike Mom—also satisfies sexual desires. Small food for thought: Have you, as a woman, ever been praised for doing the laundry?

> "A man who takes care of the laundry at home is sometimes celebrated as if he had cured breast cancer."
> Theresa Nerz, Board Member/Social Media Manager.

Women with a "yes-but" man at their side find themselves in an inner psychological dilemma: On the one hand, they do not (yet) want to risk their relationship, and on the other hand, they strive for professional advancement. I assume that these women find it particularly difficult to give their own needs and demands the same priority as their partner. This means that, psychologically, they are half a step behind their man in the private sphere, even though they often have decision-making power, the necessary resilience, and joy in responsibility at work. How can it be that these women behave so differently in the private and professional sphere? A phenomenon that the women themselves usually cannot explain. This discrepancy may be due to a loyalty conflict regarding their own parents. The image of the mother with which these women grew up is a rather passive role in the relationship, adapted to the needs of the man. Their mother subordinated her own design wishes to the father. He lived out his role as the primary member of the family. Even if the affected women have built an intellectual distance to the life plan of their own parents, the inner psychological desire to be "a good daughter" remains. Leading a completely different life than their own parents would feel like a betrayal to them.

> "The hope that the partner will give in, the danger that the dream of family will burst, and the fear of having to go through life as a single parent, coupled with the structural challenges in companies, make many women hold on to this relationship. The wasted energy for millimeter successes leads to deep exhaustion and listlessness, which also affect professional ambitions and keep women stuck in destructive relationships."
> Marianne Brandt, Coach and Organizational Developer.

Partners who lead their women into this conflict are, in my view, men with weakened self-esteem who secure themselves through traditional role models and give themselves personal significance. They think and act less in the "you" or even "we", but are more focused on themselves. They want to keep changes or decisions in their own hands. It can be assumed that they have a particular need for control and secretly fear being overtaken or left alone by their partners.

For this type of man, career-ambitious women are interesting as long as he can upgrade himself with them. This upgrade can, for example, be achieved through his support for her—which increases his feeling of superiority—or through the admiration of his friends for the woman. But the moment she loses her independence—which is inevitably the case with a child—his refusal strategies begin. Nothing remains of the former pseudo-charmer. Since the relationship was good before, the women now no longer understand the world and embark on a grueling and hurtful journey within a frustrating long-term partnership.

5 The Balancing Act between Partnership, Motherhood, and Career

> **Renate* and her "yes-but" man**
>
> Renate* meets her future husband at university, both studying chemistry. The topic of marriage only becomes relevant when her partner starts working, while Renate is still doing her doctorate. He earns well and quickly climbs the hierarchy. Renate wants to stay at the university and do research. When he brings up the topic of marriage, he says: "And when we have children, you stay at home for a few years. You're just bouncing from one temporary job to another. I earn enough for both of us." The tone was determined and dominant, completely contrary to his otherwise very pleasant nature. Renate's partner had a clear plan of how the division of tasks should be when starting a family. For Renate, the discussion had just begun. She didn't have a plan yet.
> *Name changed

Men probably have a plan to avoid falling under the wheels of life, they are afraid.

The Fear of Men and the Power of Women

Men are afraid of losing control, of being overtaken by their partners, or even being left alone. Traditional role models have nurtured the self-image of many men as the strong man. As a result, the man sees himself as the center of the world. Women who strongly orient themselves outwardly, for example by pursuing career paths, shake his image. However, I argue that the image of the self-assured man is a myth. Each generation takes the narrative of the strong, invulnerable, and self-confident man from the previous one and passes it on to the children. The narrative has been the same for millennia. But in reality, men are supported by women in everyday life: women voluntarily take on care work, thus giving men room for their careers. This role also continues in the corporate system: here too, women are the busy bees on which men build their careers. The role is even linked in both systems: at the couple level, it is the women who often emotionally support their men so that they can succeed in their jobs.

At the same time, women have power over their men, especially on an emotional level. If they did not conform to their role assignment in the private sphere, the children would be left unattended, the apartment uncleaned, Christmas parties unprepared, and many a meeting with the boss would surely turn out more negatively for the man. Women coach their men without ever billing for it. Men often follow their women in the private sphere and leave the field to them. Here they admit power to them. And on a sexual level, women have power over men through their eroticism. Yet women are slowed down and blinded by guilt inductions on an emotional level.

The Fear of Women

Guilt inductions on the part of men achieve their goal because the fear of women slows them down in the "yes-but" relationships. The stumbling block is the fear of imbalance in the partnership and its consequences. If she asserts herself, it may lead to marital strife or latent irritability of the husband. And since some of the "yes-but" men are nice on the surface (and thus less aggressive than their male peers), she convinces herself that everything is not so bad and tries to arrange herself in the partnership. In other words: she adapts and denies her needs. And the power she actually has, she does not perceive or loses in the daily confrontation. Some men have an equally high potential for aggression, but hidden and well camouflaged, women only notice when they really stand up to their full size. Then some of these men reveal their true aversion to lived equality.

> "The fear of ending up as an 'old maid' is deep-seated and is constantly fueled by the media. Even on social media, perfect relationships are often put on display."
> Theresa Nerz, Board Member/Social Media Manager.

The Pitfalls of the "Yes-But" Trap

Phrases like: "Honey, I'll let you do your thing, but…", represent a trap for many women, as the non-existent equality between the couple is not immediately recognized as such. The partner's message is formulated benevolently, but behind the benevolence hides a restriction that comes disguised: "Honey, I'm glad when you bring money home. *But* our children are still so small, they need you and then there's our dog and the big house." Sounds nice, doesn't it?

5 The Balancing Act between Partnership, Motherhood, and Career

The message behind it is a double message: Earning money is positively evaluated, but in the next sentence it is swept off the table by guilt induction. Nothing puts women under more pressure than the neediness of their own children and the looming threat of impairing the child's welfare if they do not take sufficient care of the offspring. It is their soft spot. At the couple level, men constantly work with double messages: "You can work, *but*..." These messages work especially on an emotional level and have varying degrees of impact depending on the personality structure, education, and experiences of the women.

What all messages have in common: They are not recognized as aggressive for a long time because they are nicely packaged. Women do not notice the true intention behind the messages for a long time. The messages bind women on an emotional level—to their children, but also to their partner. The difficulty lies in representing one's own or even opposing position in the face of seemingly nice messages. Often women even believe that their husband's opinion is valid—after all, they could be wrong themselves.

Let's start where everything begins, even before child and career top each other: The couple relationship with a "yes-but" man only really gets out of balance after the birth of the first child. Until then, both careers are easy to organize because there is no need to fight for the resource of time. There is no one to take care of and she probably still managed the household easily, provided he did not participate. The distribution of household chores is probably already skewed before the family is founded. After the first child, there is a landslide here. Either she sees her role from now on as a full-time mother or it comes to the classic role distribution with part-time work of the woman, which then cements over the years, or the women slide into their role—more involuntarily than actually wanted, every month a bit deeper. His support decreases over time and eventually disappears completely or it settles at a minimum: taking out the trash and putting the child to bed twice a week. Pushing the stroller a bit on Sunday, preferably while jogging.

Prerequisites for Negotiations on Compatibility

Targeted agreements on the issue of reconciling family and career can help in a partnership if several conditions are met: Women must be aware that there is something to negotiate and that their role is not divinely ordained. Rather, a traditional role distribution is essentially a millennia-old imbalance that needs to be corrected. Imbalances can be corrected by laws and regulations, but also by new strategies that break old patterns. Many women do not negotiate because they do not think of it, or because they feel comfortable in the traditional role distribution. Legislators and particularly committed women are mistaken if they think they need to champion for all women or make legal regulations. Not all women want to pursue a career. Solely caring for children and household is a desirable goal for some women. The motives underlying this goal are probably diverse: lack of female role models for an alternative, little confidence in their own competencies and abilities, fears of the "battlefield" in companies, a childhood in an educationally disadvantaged environment, the desire to be provided for by the man, convenience or indeed little interest in personal development. So there is nothing to negotiate here. Women must, in order to be able to negotiate, not only know exactly what they want—those who do not have a clear goal will conduct unclear negotiations—and they must be self-confident. Here again, self-esteem comes into play in role attributions. Those who do not value themselves enough to fight for a goal lack strength and assertiveness. Women are often confronted with fears and feelings of guilt from history, which makes the topic of negotiation even more difficult.

> Those who fear confrontations and are easily guilt-tripped will have little or nothing to counter the other party. The fear that the marriage might break up and feelings of guilt towards the seemingly neglected children are the main motives for women not to negotiate at all or not with the required stringency.

A common effect in relationships with a "yes-but" partner: The woman does achieve her set goals in such processes, but her partner eventually initiates a separation because he does not want to live with a partner on an equal footing, or a commitment only exists on paper and the reality is different.

5 The Balancing Act between Partnership, Motherhood, and Career

"At first I asked for it and wished for understanding from my husband. Then I switched to negotiating, which I could have saved myself. Finally, I got angry. My willingness to undertake fundamental changes grew during this time."
Doris Manthei, systemic family therapist and business coach.

Now let's look at the man's side, with whom negotiations are to be conducted: Apart from the fact that women are still fighting against traditional role distributions in the 21st century, the hormone level of men also plays a role. Testosterone influences the aggressive behavior of men and promotes competition and status. When women negotiate, they encounter men who have a high identification with their job. To put it bluntly: They are more keen on the office, on company cars or bonuses than on changing diapers. Because there are no privileges for performance at the changing table. Testosterone also gives them more weight in negotiation positions: a 1.85 m tall man, weighing 90 kg and with a deep voice, has a different appearance and dominance behavior than a 1.65 m tall woman. In addition, women who want to make a career come into competition with their own man: Who has the higher income, who the more luxurious company car and who the better status? And then the corporate culture of the employer also plays into the question of realization: Until the Corona pandemic, executives, usually men, were good executives if they sacrificed themselves for the company. This means 60 hours and more as a weekly working time, payment was often based on presence and not on competence or other key figures. This leads to the fact that male executives as potential partners on an equal footing could not fulfill their part simply due to lack of time. In the meantime, a different trend is emerging here, more work-life balance is in demand, also for executives.

Counterarguments in Negotiations for Compatibility
In Germany and elsewhere, the rule is: The one in the partnership who earns more money has priority in their career and is at an advantage— less money means inferiority, usually for women, because they either work in female-typical professions or actually still earn less salary than men. Childcare and household—not only the actual organization, but

also the mental juggling between the different challenges—are at the expense of women under this perspective. The regime of role assignments preferably works with guilt inductions, such as: "too much time in daycare is bad for the children", a mantra that holds incredibly well and hits women's sore points.

The role assignment is: You are the mother. This implies a reduction to the central role of a woman. Men still think it is only the woman who has the child, not both as a couple. As a rule, these arguments are put forward and hide the true intention, namely that their own career and their own professional development have priority. And some men are even glad that their partner is so busy from the birth of a common child that she no longer comes up with any "stupid ideas".

Meanwhile, employers are doing a lot to facilitate the compatibility of family and job: They also offer fathers parental leave and temporary part-time models, home office has become part of most workplaces, and dual leadership is making its way into companies. Full-day daycare and schools, household help, and au pairs can enable women's career opportunities. Parents argue with non-existent daycare places and hardly consider alternatives—because other forms of care cost more money and there is no understanding in the middle class that you can take nannies, day mothers or au pairs if the woman is professionally challenged to advance. On issues such as vacation or the purchase of a second car, however, the cost issue plays only a subordinate role. Behind this divided measure still hides the belief that the only true reference person for a child is the mother. And some women continue to believe this.

How and when do I now confront my partner with my wishes for a fairer distribution of household and child?
There is probably never a really good time to state your position and achieve negotiation successes. The best time, in my opinion, is right at the beginning of a relationship. Then, when you as a couple have to find each other and your two behavioral patterns are not yet ingrained.

Because one thing must be clear to you: It's not just about your partner contributing his part to household and childcare. It's also about you not filling the gap that arises during his domestic absence. Women tend to take over his tasks to ensure a smooth running of household and childcare. They also want to avoid conflicts and fall victim to their great sense of responsibility. And so it quickly creeps in—if there are no clear regulations to which both adhere—that she takes the main responsibility. The equal distribution of the burden also reaches its limits when women are married to men in leadership positions. Here there are time limits, because these predominantly spend more hours in the office than at home.

> **The Term Support**
>
> It's not about men *supporting* their women in household and offspring, but about a burden that needs to be fairly distributed on both shoulders. Rather use sentences like: "We live in a household, we eat from a refrigerator, we have children together, therefore we have the following tasks to accomplish together ..."

> **What to do?**
>
> The best recipe is prevention. If you have been in a "yes-but" relationship for a long time, a habituation effect occurs: everything is not so bad, after all, he never raises his voice. You trivialize. The longer you stay in the relationship, the less strength you have to break free from it. Either a full-blown crisis, such as an affair of your husband, or the emptiness after the youngest child has also moved out, etc., can help you to literally blast yourself out of the relationship. It would be better: you start questioning the messages you receive at the beginning of a relationship. Are they double messages: Yes, but ...?
>
> How does your partner react when you do the opposite, i.e., do not follow the but, but take your own position? Does he become aggressive or does he give in? You need to start testing your potential partner. And how do you react? Do you adapt to the but when, for example, a leadership position is offered to you and the new job means business trips and extra work? Do you suppress your own opinion because you are unsure? Do you have feelings of guilt or fears? Or do you negotiate?
>
> I recommend: Negotiate with your partner! If you start negotiating, there is a chance that you will eventually move on an equal footing with your partner—but only on the condition that your partner is willing and thus willing to accept you as an equal. Couples or women usually negotiate around three topics:

> - Who works how much and takes care of the children?
> - Who does the housework?
> - Who organizes social life and the private environment?

Most men do not want to deal with household management or child-rearing and organization. If you have such a partner:

- Work out a plan! A somewhat realistic plan, preferably in writing, and pin it to the refrigerator door. Take work off him and signal to him: These are your tasks, I'm sure it will work. And everything is fine!

If you have a partner who wants to participate, create a plan based on conversations. It may take several conversations, but don't give up! Especially when he signals that the family is important to him. If, on the other hand, you have a partner who persistently resists, ask yourself: What is the point of this partnership if you are left alone?

> "Prepare yourself! What is your bargaining chip, what is negotiable for you and where do you make no compromises? You should always know your worst-case scenario so that you know if and when to quit."
> Dr. Ursula Koehler, systemic coach and expert for self-empowerment.

5.2.2 We are definitely not a team: Wrong partner choice and competitive relationships

The following considerations of couple constellations are taken from the Side-by-Side study (Brandt et al. 2020):

> "You don't need a partner to be happy. Another person can never give absolute happiness if you can't give happiness to yourself. Also, don't forget, if a person really loves someone, then this person wants you to be absolutely well."
> Theresa Nerz, Board Member/Social Media Manager.

5 The Balancing Act between Partnership, Motherhood, and Career

Variant 1: Measuring forces together

> **Marina* and the consequences of starting a family**
>
> Marina* studied law and earned her doctorate in the USA. There she meets her future husband. Both do their legal clerkship and start working in large law firms at the same time. She thinks that the job in a large law firm and two children can be well combined. Far from it. Her partner is almost completely unavailable for tasks in the household and childcare. His working hours often last until 10 pm and so the marriage does not take a good course.
> *Name changed

This competitive relationship was originally chosen for quite sporting and encouraging reasons. Women in such couple constellations like the competition, the measuring of forces, the intellectual confrontation with the partner. Climbing as high as possible on the career ladder is a high goal for both. The relationship inspires them and him for their own personal and professional advancement. They are each other's sparring partners and push each other to success. Although there are competing feelings and even envy, they are seen more as a stimulating element in the competition.

Competitive Partnership as a Career Obstacle So, everything seems fine? Basically, yes. But the imbalance for this couple begins with starting a family. Only in starting a family does it become apparent whether the couple is also a team. Having a desire for children and then living this life with the necessary continuity and flexibility are two different things. Intellectually, it is rather boring for both to engage with children.

It turns out that women then feel obliged, often out of guilt, to offer something to their children: time, attention, immersing themselves in the world of children, dealing with parent-teacher meetings and nutritional issues, even if it does not correspond to their intellectual interests. Meanwhile, the man continues to pursue his career ambitions, especially if he is already further along in his career than she is and could have foregone children for his life planning.

The couple loses its original sense of community and falls by the wayside due to the family imbalance and the increasingly apparent aggression. For the women, this means additional efforts to continue pursuing their own career. Because they are tied up in daily annoyance and the feeling of being abandoned by their partner.

> "He said his working time was too valuable, he couldn't also take care of children and household."
> A participant in the Side-by-Side study 2020.

Recognized Too Late Ultimately, women in this pair constellation have put themselves in a dead end with the idea that career and family can be combined on an equal footing with their partner. The couple failed to build a new mindset in their relationship that would have allowed both to pursue their career path in fair play. In these relationships, traditional ideas (mothers are responsible for the children, men pursue careers) often unconsciously prevail, which only become apparent with the founding of a family—too late for these women. These partnerships are extremely fragile and prone to divorce.

Variant 2: I have you under control

Renate* and her "Controller"

Renate* has built a company with more than 100 employees on her own. She is a top entrepreneur and a strong woman. But her marriage is a disaster. She is controlled by her husband: When does she leave the house? When should she be back? When do her meetings end and in which hotel does she stay during business trips? He calls and spies on her, and is also jealous. After business dinners, she is questioned at home: Who were you dining with? Why did it take so long?
  *Name changed

In this competitive relationship, a special dependency phenomenon prevails between the couple. On the outside, everything seems to be fine. The woman is very successful, runs companies, makes tough decisions, is top in her field. She shows herself to be autonomous in

5 The Balancing Act between Partnership, Motherhood, and Career

confrontations and fully capable in the male-dominated decision-making world. Her partner remains rather in the background. Perhaps he is also very successful himself or just "only" the husband of a successful woman.

Both types of men show little public presence with their women and do not support them. They are surrounded by a certain flair as "grey eminences". For the outside world, this is not particularly impressive, as these women stand for themselves.

Behind Closed Doors

In fact, these women find themselves in a power-impotence constellation in relation to their partners. They are extremely susceptible to their partners' criticism—and they hear a lot of it. Their self-esteem and self-respect are systematically undermined, like a steady drip that wears away the stone. It is symptomatic that women in emotional dependencies try to meet the demands of their men. They systematically isolate themselves from the outside world, i.e., their partner ensures that they have no own circle of friends, no best friend, and no intimate conversation and exchange opportunities. He controls them at work and in private life. All this happens subtly and behind closed doors.

> "And then he said: What you do and with whom, I decide!"
> A participant in the Side-by-Side study 2020.

Fed from Deep Abysses

At the couple level, we are talking about subtle violence systems in these cases, which can be understood from our history (see transgenerational transmission). It would be a mistake to believe that this phenomenon only works with weak or insecure women. Especially the successful and capable women are at risk, especially if they come from very strict or even violent families of origin. For their partners, it is a special sign of personal greatness to be able to successfully control these strong women.

Such constellations solidify as the women obey their partners' prohibitions and also deny their inner psychological dependency. Unfortunately, with fatal consequences, because this is how these power-impotence systems continue to function, often over many decades.

For the affected women, this life means a tremendous energetic and psychological effort.

What Keeps the Women?
Why don't these intelligent and reflective women see the situation they are in? I do not rule out that these women do know or at least suspect over the years that they are entangled in unhealthy, dysfunctional power relations. Often, children are involved, who prevent them from leaving, and what should not be underestimated from a psychological point of view: This way of living is deeply familiar to these women from their own history.

5.2.3 The Ideal Case: "Honey, I'm in!"—The Couple as a Team

> **Sybille* and the man by her side**
>
> Sybille* and Ernst* live the team spirit. She is a manager in a large corporation, she was offered a three-year stay abroad. Her husband works as a freelance journalist and can work from anywhere. For him, it is clear that his wife's career takes precedence. He thinks she is more competent and ambitious. They are supported by an au pair who will look after their four-year-old daughter. Both see no problem in this constellation.
> *Names changed

Despite all the disillusioning statements that underlie the way out of the regiment of role assignments, it remains to be noted: There are also men who want to support their partners' careers. Whether necessary relocations, stays abroad or the question of childcare—relevant questions are openly addressed and concessions to the woman's career are actively lived. The professional advancement of these men does not seem to be at the center of their personal focus, their focus is rather on the chance to realize a common life plan with their partner.

> "My boyfriend says: You are the better of us two. You make the career!"
> A participant of the Side-by-Side study 2020.

Partnership with Children

In this relationship constellation, women are usually the (main) breadwinners of the family. This is also clarified and desired in the internal relationship. However, the women also reported in the Side-by-Side study (Brandt et al. 2020) that their men do indeed experience phases in which they feel bad and their own self-esteem plummets. However, it is also characteristic of these couples that this state is changeable and both are ready to actively deal with it.

Despite the economic imbalance between (main) breadwinner and partner, the relationship is seen as a joint project with a common success strategy.

There are also equally career-ambitious couple relationships in which both want to exploit their professional opportunities. In these relationships, a good balance between professional advancement and family needs and desires is taken into account, sometimes in the form of "right of way rules"—in the sense of: "Honey, now it's your turn."

What Makes These Relationships So Strong

Such challenges, desires for change or also necessities are openly addressed in the partnership. Solutions are sought and found together. Both partners see themselves as a team, in which each has a claim to personal development and unfolding.

These relationships are characterized by stability and reliability, but also by flexibility and willingness to change. Positive experiences from their own family of origin strengthen this couple.

> "My husband has the right self-confidence to be the way he is."
> A participant of the Side-by-Side study 2020.

When the Couple Does Not Yet Have Children

For young women who do not yet have children, however, a certain X-factor remains despite all the positive experiences already lived, namely to what extent the common plans and agreements can also be realized when children come into play. How will they experience their motherhood? Do they feel more bound to the child than they thought beforehand? Will the partner really go along with it?

This risk is manageable for them. The confidence to find solutions together that can make both possible—family and career—is high.

A Role Model with a Future

This team-couple type is certainly not yet the norm, neither in society as a whole nor anchored as a self-evident life model in the respective families. Corresponding messages and irritations from the environment can therefore represent an additional burden for young couples in particular. The challenge for this couple is to build an inner distance and understand that it is not about fulfilling the wishes and ideas of the environment.

In my estimation, this is particularly successful for those women (couples) who were either able to experience a similar role model from their family of origin or whose parents strengthened the professional development aspirations of their daughters. They do not have to feed their self-esteem from role stereotypes or status thinking, but can be a couple on an equal footing.

Wrong Partner as a Knockout for the Career

The fact is: If you want to make a career as a woman and want to live in a heterosexual partnership, you need a career-compatible man. The wrong choice of partner is one of the biggest knockout criteria for female careers. Most women do not think about whether their partner can positively or negatively influence their career. They rather look for a partner who in attitude and behavior resembles their father, because this type is familiar to them and inspires trust. In addition: The hormone status of women is trimmed for reproduction and thus also determines the choice of partner. Women do not look for a man who supports their career, but a supposedly strong man who can father healthy children and protect the family.

This deeply archaic and biological process runs as an unconscious program. As a result, women lose sight of important questions: What is my partner's attitude towards career? Does he want children? Who will take care of these to what parts? What about stays abroad? Is he willing to step back professionally in favor of my career? To get ahead, women don't need a "yes-but" partner, but clear concessions: "I am willing to step back for you and our children."

In the first phase of falling in love, a cocktail of hormones is released that blurs the view of the facts. In the rush of dopamine and oxytocin, the partner's behaviors in the context of equality are either not actually seen or denied, according to the motto: "I can still get a handle on them." Even a man who suits you has characteristics and beliefs that can contradict your needs.

> **What to do?**
> Even in the phase of infatuation, you should try to stay on the factual level when choosing a partner. Do a partner check: A man who supports your career is not enough. For the realization of your career, you need someone who shares the time for childcare and household chores with you. In short: A partnership on an equal footing.
>
> To take up a powerful leadership position in the job, you need a fair distribution of care work or appropriate external support. Otherwise, you will lack not only time and energy to fulfill both satisfactorily, but also the representation of your own interests. You lay the foundation for your career prospects at the beginning of a relationship: Anyone who does not negotiate and represent their interests here will probably not do so in the company with few exceptions!

5.3 Excursus: Partner Search and Motherhood

5.3.1 Partner Search on an Equal Footing

So that you don't even get into the situation of having to stand up for yourself and your needs and having to fight hard for it, we should focus on how women find a suitable partner who neither keeps them small nor wants to "soften" them, points out their mother role and leaves them alone with it in everyday life. Let's look at the topic from the other side: Which woman will a man choose who is looking for a partner on an equal footing? A conformist? One drilled for obedience? A woman who cannot feed herself and is looking for a provider? Or a woman who also has something to offer intellectually? What do you think? I assume that these types of men are looking for independent, financially and emotionally independent women who are firmly rooted in life, i.e., have a good self-esteem. Because these men, unlike their male peers, have different expectations of a partnership: They are looking for a sparring partner, i.e., a woman who shares the burden of daily life financially and emotionally and with whom they can also exchange ideas on an intellectual level.

This is where, in my opinion, the dilemma of women begins, because many of them are still looking for a provider or father 2.0 or feel worthless themselves (see Sect. 2.2). The bad news: The number of men looking for partners on an equal footing is small, i.e., the partner selection for women is limited. This inevitably leads to women who are looking for a partner on an equal footing passing by potential candidates—they do not meet, neither statistically nor on an emotional level. Suitable men do not dock.

You probably suspect it: The search for such a partner begins with working on yourself! And this work includes taking on personal responsibility, namely for whether your career as a woman can succeed thanks to the right partner choice and adequate handling of motherhood. The sad reality: At both decisive milestones of their life, women do not take good or any care of themselves. There are obstacles to why the partnership of a career-ambitious woman does not succeed—and unfortunately, she often does not ensure that it can at least theoretically succeed, because she does not create the basic prerequisites for it.

> **Deal with the following questions**
>
> Ask yourself:
>   Am I ready to stand my ground as a woman or do I want to be provided for?
>   Do I see myself as valuable? Do I "deserve" a partner on an equal footing?
>   Do I always choose partners who resemble my father? What behavioral patterns, characteristics, etc. attract me and then turn out to be negative for me?
>   How do I actually want to live a partnership on an equal footing? Do I have concrete ideas or are these vague and fulfill a role?

5 The Balancing Act between Partnership, Motherhood, and Career

"No question, women want to earn their own money. But when I ask them if they are ready to feed their family, they start to hesitate. Here, an invisible trap usually snaps shut, namely that of the classic role assignment. Because women usually still assign the role of the main earner to their partner. This role assignment expresses their inner attitude of wanting to be provided for in the common standard of living by putting their own career on hold or giving up."

Marianne Brandt, coach and organizational developer.

Searching for an Equal Partner

Let's turn to the classic characteristics of men who are on an equal footing: I recommend looking for men who are factually compatible and therefore also exhibit certain traits. What do I mean by that?

If you, as a woman, have career ambitions and you meet a "leader man", it could be that you have not found a partner compatible with your life concept. Men in leadership positions are hard to spare time-wise, i.e., a fair distribution of household and childcare will not exist simply due to the lack of time. And the idea that alpha males would give up career, status, and income, I find unlikely. A parental leave for the duration of two months or one evening per week for childcare might be feasible for some of these men, but you are still far from a fair distribution of care work and domestic duties. In addition, these men usually have a high identification with their job. So, do not expect voluntary reduction of working hours and more engagement in an area where there are no merits. Make it clear: childcare and household management are not in the interest of these men! Successfully getting them there with societal pressure or corporate measures, I consider an illusion.

Career-Ambitious Women Must

- look for men who do not strive for power and leadership, thus are less ambitious;
- be willing themselves to take on the role of breadwinner, or
- have a clear consensus with their partner that all matters of household management and childcare are outsourced—to service providers, daycare, and all-day schools.

Characteristics of men on an equal footing include showing little to no dominance. They can adapt well to the needs of women, step back, and have a certain degree of empathy. They can empathize well with the needs of their partner and later also with the needs of their children. Usually, they are rather quiet, inconspicuous men who do not need to push themselves into the foreground and do not necessarily go openly on the hunt for women. Men on an equal footing distance themselves from the sexist remarks of their male peers and have a democratic understanding of relationships, hence their potential for aggression is inevitably low. Violence is alien to them, they seek fulfillment and benevolent relationships.

The Burden of Growing Responsibility
Even men who manage to act on an equal footing in the partnership until the first child is born may want to shirk the responsibility for household and childcare with an increasing number of children. Even after a promising partner check result, there can be a break here after the birth of the first child.

And just because a man wants a child or more does not mean that he also strives to take on the corresponding responsibility. Many men want to prove their masculinity through the number of their children, nothing more. They only realize late that life as a working family father does not correspond to what they had promised themselves.

5.3.2 Motherhood and the Traps and Illusions of Women

With one child or several children, some women realize a dream of life, they have reached their goal, they think. Women are deceived by a false world, not only through fairy tales at the bedside, but also through media, especially social media and advertising. A perfect world is staged for young girls, culminating in motherhood. About the way there and what the dream actually looks like, society remains silent. Reality makes the vision appear in a different light: Women in their young years do not think about whether the partner is compatible with their career

5 The Balancing Act between Partnership, Motherhood, and Career

wishes, nor do they think about the consequences of children. Instead, they follow their feelings and hormones, less their rationality. And at this point, the question of responsibility comes into play again.

> "'That's not love if I approach everything so rationally,' women often object. Perhaps self-love begins here when women make clear what they want. When they develop an attitude for themselves and their ideas despite all the butterflies in their stomach and stand up for it. This does not exclude romance."
> Marianne Brandt, Coach and Organizational Developer.

Young women do not yet understand the pitfalls of development that prioritizing a mother role brings. But when the partner reorients himself in the midlife crisis and the children have flown the nest, a feeling of lack sets in. The previous life concept falls short, the decreasing hormone level in the climacteric further intensifies the feeling of increasing insignificance and decreasing attractiveness. Now the topic of job and career gains importance again—either to fill the void or the bank account. The perceived pain becomes the drive. However, those who have pushed their own career from the beginning without a cooperative partner and without a support system, lose a lot: no time for themselves, but an eternal balancing act between career, child, man, household, and extended family at the expense of their own strength. In both life paths, women do not take enough responsibility for themselves. Their life revolves too much around others, they do not put themselves in the center and do not take care of their own resources or needs. They define themselves through the well-being of their family, not through their own well-being. So, when it comes to motherhood, women do not take good care of themselves. And with the wrong partner choice and the hurdles of motherhood, the fragile power in their hands slips away.

Children as Self-Worth Assurance and Emotional Old-Age Provision
Women distance themselves from their desires and needs as soon as they become mothers. From then on, they pursue an ideal image of motherhood shaped by upbringing, beliefs, and environment in the context of career and

partnership. Influencers further support this glorification. Essentially, their emotional life hinders women from their own career. Because guilt, shame, fear, and insecurity accompany their thinking and actions as (working) mothers. Women's self-worth is still too often tied to the care of their children and the associated external recognition or to meeting all expectations perfectly. Women need the feeling of being needed, especially emotionally. Therefore, for many women, children are an emotional old-age provision, often unconsciously. The offspring are supposed to compensate for their own emotional deficits or alleviate the fear of aging, distract from an unhappy partnership, or give the feeling of finally being loved unconditionally. But this love is usually unconditional only until puberty. Then the offspring turn away—and what was supposed to be compensated for is painfully present at the latest.

The Waning Power of Mothers

The secret power of women lies in caring for the family. Through their role as mothers, they gain power over the family. This compensates them for the lack of power externally—even if this power leaves much to be desired in terms of money, recognition, and prestige. However, it dissolves, among other things, with the process of children's detachment. Powerful jobs in the family system may temporarily increase self-worth, but the loss of associated tasks extinguishes this power and cannot be revived at this level.

Lack of Self-Understanding for Outsourcing Care Work

On the subject of motherhood, women seem to split into two camps: those who want to follow the traditional path—for me a phenomenon of retraditionalization—and those who want to reconcile career and family or even a career in top management with family. Both groups have in common that children are seen as the meaning of life.

But those who want to reconcile career and children have different approaches depending on their origin and current social status. While it is quite common in the upper class to send their offspring to boarding school or to use the help of au pairs, housekeepers, or gardeners to meet family needs while parents pursue their own career, the German middle class lacks self-understanding here. There is no consistent awareness that the service of childcare can be integrated as a fixed part of family life beyond the offers of daycare and after-school care, to allow flexibility in the job for both. It is not only the cost issue that stands in the way of implementation, but also the limited perspective of the social milieu, which is still oriented towards traditional role assignments. There is no exchange between the milieus, so there are no cross-milieu role models here.

The following remarks on career-ambitious and performance-willing women in the context of motherhood are taken from the Side-by-Side study (Pamminger et al. 2020):

Career-ambitious women usually do not withdraw from the job when they have children, but return after maternity leave. Even young women who do not yet have children usually plan a quick return. Part-time or full-time? Both models are conceivable for them.

> "When you hear: 'This is only possible full-time', then I think: And why? It's just a blockage in the head, why it shouldn't work."
> A participant in the Side-by-Side study 2020.

For these women, it is a matter of course that even the highest management levels can be managed with two or more children. But so far, there are only a few top female managers in this country who are able to reconcile two or more children with their job. As already mentioned, this usually only works with the support of their partner or external service providers such as nannies, au pairs, etc. Regarding the question of what role children play in shaping their own career, the following aspects are striking:

Top Women

> **Susanne* and Corporate Culture**
>
> Susanne* is a top woman, manager of a pharmaceutical company. Business trips, evening meetings, and two children have made her tired. After an accident and the subsequent forced break, she resigns—completely unexpected for her company. The cause: incompetent superiors, increasing listlessness, and constant quarrels at work. Susanne no longer wants this job.
>   *Name changed

Top women, who are extremely committed, work at a very high pace and 70 to 80 hours a week, live in the fast lane. These women want to participate at the top of the power centers and they pursue this goal very consistently. Even serious physical and mental stress symptoms are ignored by them. They miss their children's lives and gradually alienate themselves from them. In the long run, this effort is hardly sustainable physically and emotionally.

Even if this behavior is generally postulated as a path to success, I see it as a disturbance of self-regulation due to permanently high external stimuli. This miscontrol behavior can affect men and women alike. Ultimately, these high performers are in a dependency spiral, in which they are driven by the special fascination of work, a high willingness to perform, and a self-worth definition dependent on the success achieved.

Particularly profound, emotional experiences can lead those affected out of this process and enable a new balance. These can be painful experiences, such as one's own serious illness or that of family members, but also completely unexpected experiences that trigger new decisions.

> "A defining event was when I wanted to pick up my child from kindergarten and had to show my ID."
> A participant of the Side-by-Side study 2020.

Also, the missed life in their own family, the worry that their children might suffer from the mother's absence and develop behavioral problems, as well as the deep feeling that they can never catch up on the missed developments of their children, can make top women on the fast track reconsider. They are even willing to take a career setback if the company does not show flexibility towards them.

Women make these decisions, even if it sets them back many years in their career and they have significantly less money. To do without these top women means letting many unused years pass by—less for the women, as they know their personal gain—but rather for the companies.

> "Until I retire at 75, I can still make a lot of career."
> A participant of the Side-by-Side study 2020.

Factor Leadership and Corporate Culture

Questioning the leadership culture in the company is a "hot potato". In one-on-one conversations, men are usually open and see the leadership culture in the company quite critically. But when it comes to changes in the leadership culture, it often doesn't fit—important other projects, the colleagues on the board or crises have priority. The hot potato is dropped and corresponding personnel programs are reduced to a minimum.

Performance-oriented Women

> **Marianne* and her Boss**
>
> Marianne* has a double degree, has a doctorate and now only works twelve hours a week. After the second child, she wanted more flexible working hours, home office and further training opportunities. She had long discussions with her supervisor, who proved to be inflexible and rigid. This led Marianne to reduce her working hours. She is no longer motivated to make a special effort for this employer.
> *Name changed

In addition to the top female managers, there is a group of equally high-performing women who, however, prefer a balance between work and family from the start of their career. Having and accompanying children is an important part of their life plan, but they are also willing to continue to demonstrate their commitment and willingness to perform for the company, even with a family. However, they can and want to no longer work overtime to the usual extent and spend long evening hours at work, but only work part-time.

Women report how they were systematically excluded in the company after their return from maternity leave and increasingly experienced themselves as a "persona non grata". They see themselves on the sidetrack and not recognized in their loyalty to the company.

> "I was no longer asked about tasks. You're no longer on the radar."
> A participant of the Side-by-Side study 2020.

The result: They quit. This does not happen without aggression towards the employer. The revenge of these women consists in the withdrawal of their own performance.

Even young women who do not yet have children can develop a similar motivation to refuse the employer. For example, when they have to find out that they are kept in the waiting loop with empty promises despite excellent performance.

> "A friend put it exactly like this: If your career isn't progressing anyway, then have a child."
> A participant of the Side-by-Side study 2020.

The reasons for these behaviors are certainly understandable, but they also show the dysfunctional dynamics between the women and their superiors. Open conversations no longer take place due to the inner injury on the part of the women. They show their emotional involvement by absence and turn to their children and private life.

> "Today I only work 12 hours, which is crazy considering my qualifications."
> A participant of the Side-by-Side study 2020.

In 2020, according to the Federal Statistical Office, about two-thirds of all working mothers (65.5%) worked part-time, while only 7.1% of fathers did. This ratio reflects the prevailing regiment of role assignments: Women are primarily sought as mothers and secondarily as labor, not the other way around.

In my opinion, there are far too few efforts on the part of companies to change this ratio. Instead of tapping the potential of well-educated mothers with a corresponding personnel policy, the call for skilled workers from abroad is loud. In addition, working for these women under the constant pressure to fulfill the assigned role is usually "devoid of pleasure". Ambitions are quietly buried, the rotten compromise is sold to oneself and others as a good solution for the sake of the children. At the same time, sticking to a part-time job is also a testament to a lack of personal responsibility—where there is a lack of a sufficient

5 The Balancing Act between Partnership, Motherhood, and Career

income for one's own livelihood, partners and possibly the state should provide the necessary balance. This view is still being nurtured by society.

What weighs heavily here is the issue behind it: the narrative of the raven mother who abandons her children. And what takes the perversion of the system to the extreme: The accusation of being a raven mother as a career-oriented mother is not only raised by men, but also by fellow women such as friends, colleagues, mothers and mothers-in-law, teachers and kindergarten educators. There is little to no solidarity among women.

> To put it bluntly: Where power would exist if women allied, they lose power because they fight each other.

The Bad Mother

The natural desire for one's own career cannot be represented and lived by career-minded women, neither internally nor towards their environment. The fear of being a bad mother if they admit to their ambitions is, in my estimation, still widespread among many women.

Why is this so?

The term has persisted in Germany since the "Mother's Order" time of National Socialism. One must assume that something that lasts so long and is reused in a society makes sense—not for women, but in the context of the topic behind it. You are certainly familiar with the term German Angst (see Bode 2016). Germans are a fearful people (see transgenerational transmissions, Sect. 2.1). Anyone who wants to keep a people in check in a democracy without using undemocratic methods works with fear. Fear becomes a method, a tool of society, to keep women in check in this specific case. A woman who believes she is a bad mother if she does not sacrifice herself is a willing woman who can be easily controlled. And nothing generates more guilt in women than the issue of irresponsibility towards their children.

The traditional women: I don't have children to then pursue a career

> **Ursula* and the joy of motherhood**
> Ursula* is looking forward to her first child. Her husband earns well and is on his way to becoming a top executive. Ursula has studied, but has little ambition. At the moment, she is completely focused on the upcoming birth. What comes after is of little interest to her.
>   *Name changed

These women also exist. Their common statement that children and career are incompatible is a verbal reprimand to those women who want to develop professionally and make a lot of effort to make the balancing act between child and career work.

Why do some women think this way?

For me, there are only two explanations: There are women who act like "mother animals" because they have pronounced maternal feelings and whose purpose in life is to have children and raise them. A life without children is unimaginable for them because it is the (almost) only content of life.

Behind these women are still insecure women who take the path of least resistance and unreflectively meet the role expectations of their partner and society. Unreflective, because they give little to no thought to what the regiment of role assignment ultimately means for them. An almost naive path—no personal life concept, no plan, no goals, but instead following the prescribed path of a patriarchal society. The lack of reflection of these women is accompanied by the attitude of a patriarchal system that neither appreciates nor truly tolerates the letting go and delegating of childcare, for example by using childcare facilities or nannies. For many women, a child therefore means a power and balancing act that will never fully work. As a result, women prefer to take care of child-rearing completely rather than half-heartedly doing their job.

However, all the women described have in common that women develop more or less feelings of guilt when it comes to their children.

5 The Balancing Act between Partnership, Motherhood, and Career

The Greatest Fear of Women
The fear of perhaps not providing enough care, intensity, or duration for their children, and possibly applying wrong parenting methods, means high-performance stress for women. Because if something goes wrong, for example in the form of poor school grades, or the offspring becomes noticeable in other ways, it is primarily the mothers who are held responsible. The reason is quickly found: too much career, too little time at home, not cooking healthily, etc. But the stress is based on more than platitudes: Women have built a highly emotional relationship with their child due to their pregnancy and birth—feelings that a man cannot understand, which cannot be blamed on him due to his different biological disposition. Women release bonding hormones, such as oxytocin, during childbirth, which ensure the survival of the infant. Raising children is no walk in the park: it means sleepless nights, sore nipples, 24-hour availability on call, and perhaps even postnatal depression.

> "I think it's important to know this. And if you know it, you can deal with it consciously. I mentally perceived it as 'work' to go back to the office after a short time: to make clear which feelings (hormones) are at work, means at the same time to make clear that there is absolutely no objective reason why the child should be worse off if the father(!) stays at home. This required a plan, a clear goal, and the willingness to commit to something that not only optimizes one's own emotional state, but the entire family system. In short: summer vacations are always nicer than no summer vacations, but I still know that there is no life with eternal summer vacations."
> Daniela Mündler, founder and managing director.

Furthermore, children are primarily cared for by women from infancy, leading to the child's fixation on the mother and not the father. The imprinting in the first months of life therefore takes place on the mother. The relationship between mother and child is thus strengthened—but so strongly that the mother remains the most important person of reference until puberty, if not even into young adulthood. This means: She remains responsible, on the factual as well as on the emotional level. She provides comfort, helps overcome many crises and hurdles, conveys security, and turns her children into social beings—because she promotes the ability to relate and bond through closeness and empathy, thus creating the basic prerequisite for psychological stability.

And then men bring the societal image of the good mother into play and play, consciously or unconsciously, with women's feelings of guilt. If they (or traditionally minded peers) doubt with their statements that the woman is a good mother due to her career orientation, women deviate from their professional plans and goals to have more time for their children.

> "Women are under pressure in several respects: There are massive expectations of women regarding their role as women and mothers. The societal contribution of women is comparatively little recognized because the relationship, care, or educational work predominantly performed by women in their professional or private lives does not have the deserved status in society. High work time demands make a balance between private life and job difficult to reconcile, especially in leadership positions. Mothers in particular find themselves in a situation where they are constantly trying to meet all expectations, which leads to overburdening, or they sacrifice their desire for a career, which can also be a disadvantageous decision for them. Instead of the question of priorities or the decision for child or career, it is about the integration of family and childcare, which is not only a highly personal but also a societal concern. We need a growing family-friendly or family-integrating work culture within our economic or corporate system that allows men and women alike to be included and to grow into a new flexible role and task distribution."
> Michaela Kay, consultant and board member.

The completely exaggerated image of the mother persists stubbornly in Germany, it is cherished and nurtured. It feeds on studies that want to prove with scientific tools how and under what conditions a daycare center is even an option for children. Too early and too long separation from the mother is difficult, especially male researchers tell women. At the same time, other studies claim to have found that early attendance at a daycare center is good for child development. Every year a "new pig", i.e. a new study, is driven through the village, what is good or bad for children. To this mix, radiant mothers in social media channels join in, shining with how great they are and under what conditions their own offspring turn out wonderfully. Here, women are shown a perfect world. And it has an effect on women: They believe it.

> "Images and messages always have an effect! Even if we don't listen consciously, perceived information goes directly to the subconscious like on a highway and stays there. It's a kind of hypnosis, permanent and everywhere (advertising, social media, TV, cinema)."
> Dr. Ursula Koehler, systemic coach and expert for self-empowerment.

Women seem extremely insecure about the quality of their educational performance. Burdened with feelings of guilt and fears, they exhibit behaviors that often run counter to their own needs—driven by the desire not to do anything wrong. Actually, I should write at this point: Parents are very insecure. But it is de facto the mothers who primarily take care of the quality of education and take responsibility. Fathers take care of pick-up and drop-off services, parental duties in the soccer club, etc., but the emotional care for the children is still a woman's job.

> The image of the self-sacrificing good mother can only be maintained because women submit to it. They let partners, parents, daycare educators, friends, teachers, and scientists tell them how they should be to be a good mother. Because they either have no gut feeling or do not trust the feeling of what would really be good for their child, or do not make the effort to question how much mother their child actually needs, or give more credence to supposed experts.

Who or what does your child need?

Every child is unique, just like the mother herself. Children are born with certain character traits. They develop based on their already established personality type. A delicate and fearful child can eventually become a person who has learned to cope with their fears. Seemingly strong on the outside, fearful on the inside. To truly understand what your child needs in terms of closeness and attention, and then to decide how much daycare and how much career your child can handle, you need to know your child very well. Is your child a very strong child and wants to explore the world early on, or is it fearful and prefers to stay close to you?

And you need to know yourself. A mother is not necessarily a good mother when she gives up her career to fully devote herself to the child. A good mother is also not a mother who imposes herself on the child and constantly crosses boundaries to nourish herself through the over-closeness to the child. Some mothers have strong emotional deficits, unfulfilled longings, which are not covered by their own husband, so they need their children more than the children need them. To put it bluntly: they abuse them. The boundaries of abuse are fluid, there is no rule here. It is not always the daycare and long care times that are to blame for a child's behavioral problems and issues, but the overprotection and deficits of the parents, the constant boundary violations and threats. Often in this context, the accusation of neglect is raised. But neglect does not necessarily mean letting the child be cared for in facilities instead of taking care of it yourself, but neglect begins, for example, with an uncovered breakfast table, with disinterest in school matters up to psychological and physical or even sexualized violence. Children need reliable and constant caregivers, but not necessarily the mother or father all day. Grandparents and loving nannies can also become reliable caregivers—if women overcome their dilemma and practice letting go and trusting that other caregivers than themselves are also capable of giving their children what they need.

The own partner is often not good enough for some women in terms of educational performance, they practically push him out. Women feel threatened in their territory, their self-esteem often depends on the care work. Their unfulfilled longings for closeness and the unrestricted love of their children make it difficult for women to let go. The parade sentence: "I don't have a child to then pursue a career", is the killer par excellence, because it makes it impossible for women to stay with themselves. If it turned out that men can do the care work just as well, this realization would bring a weakening of female self-esteem with it.

5 The Balancing Act between Partnership, Motherhood, and Career

> **Consider the following questions**
> Who is your child—how much mother does your child really need?
> Who are you? What do your children stand for in your life?
> How much trust do you place in your partner or other caregivers? Is your constant presence and attention really necessary?

The goal of this questioning is that you do not succumb to the temptation to self-sacrifice for your child. The temptation to distance yourself from yourself and your needs is a huge danger in the child question because the process extends over years. When you have fully understood with all the consequences that you have lost yourself, the way back to you is a very long, laborious path. I want to spare you this.

> A woman who tends to sacrifice herself is not a powerful woman. She lets circumstances, the environment, and her emotions drive and guide her—and does not take responsibility for her own well-being.

What does this mean in practice?
Your partner can also take good care of and educate your offspring if you allow or demand it. However, this also means that you should not define your self-worth and purpose in life solely through your child.

A daycare center does not have to be bad for your child if the care ratio is right and there are loving caregivers. Likewise, full-day care in infancy or toddlerhood does not necessarily lead to noticeable behavioral problems in your child. The development is directly dependent on whether your child is a fearful child or a child who wants to conquer the world, and whether you can let it go. The use of an au pair or another nanny does not automatically mean that your child will be neglected or that you as a mother will not recognize yourself at some point. The consequences depend on the personality of the caregiver and how much affection and attention you still give to the child. Just because you are a full-time or part-time mother does not mean that you are a good mother. Time is not synonymous with the quality of educational performance.

The argument that additional care or a full-day daycare center are unaffordable is only true for certain classes or only at the current time. The priorities for spending money often depend on status symbols. As a rule, well-earning middle-class families have two cars. Money is usually sufficient for good or very good German car brands or at least two vacations a year (at least until inflation has struck). Money for additional care services is theoretically available if the priorities are different. In addition, women who aspire to leadership positions are increasingly earning more. This means that the argument of financing is static and does not take into account future earning opportunities.

The hormone status after birth, which guarantees the bond between mother and child, decreases over time. This also means that the intensity of emotions decreases as the children get older. At some point, your child will no longer need you. Therefore, think about your future in financial, but also emotional terms today. In addition to missing pension entitlements, some women experience a sense of emptiness when the children leave the nest. Then finding your way back into the profession, preferably at the same level or in a similar field, becomes difficult. Development is progressing so quickly that you can lose touch after a short time and can only return to a job far below your qualifications.

What apparently made women happy in their mother role, namely their children, loses its effect because reality catches up with them at some point: behavioral problems, school difficulties, puberty with drugs and alcohol, and the former prince on the white horse has transformed: into a man with quirks, deficits, and weaknesses.

> **What needs to be done?**
> - Don't just take care of others' needs, but especially your own resources. Stop being a passenger in your life's airplane and become the pilot!
> - Practice distancing yourself from your own emotional world when it comes to decisions like choosing a partner, having children, planning your career, or caring for relatives. Orient yourself to the fact check: What long-term consequences do your decisions have?
> - No hasty decisions just because the biological clock is ticking louder and louder! Ask yourself: What is the desired child supposed to represent? Why do I need this child?

- When planning your family, realistically consider how much child you can really integrate well into your life and when overload threatens.
- Secure as much support as you really need to reconcile child and career—from your partner, from your social environment, through additional caregivers. Also admit to others the competence to take good care of your offspring and create a sustainable network!
- Agree and demand not only support from your partner, but also 50 percent participation in the organization of household and child!
- You are not helplessly exposed to the criticism of your environment: Do not allow your parents and in-laws to constantly criticize your career negatively. Demand acceptance and above all: Accept yourself as you are! If you are plagued with feelings of guilt, this is an unconscious invitation to others to criticize you.

5.4 Excursion: Large Family Instead of Small Family

What motivates women to decide whether they want to have children at all and how many? The decision is usually related to their own upbringing. If I, as a mother, grew up in a large family and found it enriching, I will strive for a large family. If I grew up as an only child and suffered from loneliness, I will want more than one child. If I experienced my siblings as burdensome and family as a millstone, then I will probably forego children.

Another deciding factor is the societal image: When is a family considered a family? It is accepted that a married couple is not a family, a couple with one child is incomplete. So, two children are good. From three children onwards, in certain circles, it is already considered an antisocial family, in the upper class it is said that he/she can afford so many children.

The family question is an emotional area. These decisions have little to do with facts—and usually just as little to do with a sober view of the coming decades under the premise of combining family and career: What do two children mean in financial and emotional terms today, tomorrow, and in 20 years? What does this mean for my pension entitlements? Could two children possibly lead me to burnout? Do I have any support or even an equal distribution of burdens?

The consequences of a lack of reflection on what the decision for a child or children entails are the wrong choice of partner for fatherhood, years of total exhaustion, and ultimately even old-age poverty or a very modest retirement existence. Because women at this milestone of their lives have not thought fact-based and thus missed the chance for a powerful position in their own lives.

In the course of pregnancy and childbirth, however, a solution must be found in relation to child and job. For many women, part-time work is then the means of choice.

At first glance, this seems to be a good solution in terms of work-life balance. But many women then find it difficult to get out of the part-time solution, especially with several children. They remain dependent on their partner and also pay little into the pension fund. The societal trend is increasingly towards work-life balance and thus towards a life concept with part-time work models, also for fathers. This can be understood as a counter-reaction to a capitalist system that has "spit out" anyone who was not willing to deliver maximum performance—at least in terms of presence. By the way, this also affects men. Men who want to participate equally in upbringing have so far not recommended themselves as top executives from the perspective of many companies. New work models like joint leadership, which envisages job sharing at management level, are still very rare in German companies.

What Would Be a Good Solution?
For me, the solution lies in the restructuring of remuneration systems. We should think about remuneration systems based on target achievement and key figures. I am aware that this is not an easy process, especially when the entire salary is controlled by it. However, it would be worth thinking about it. Especially women, due to the organizational pressure of their family situation, often work more goal-oriented and focused than men and accomplish comparable work in half the time. They invest less energy and time in networking and evening events. Opportunities that men mainly use to form cliques to advance their careers. To get work done efficiently, however, you first need people

5 The Balancing Act between Partnership, Motherhood, and Career

who work focused, not people who are primarily busy building networks during their working hours. A system under the premise of target achievement would be fairer and more family-compatible.

Unfortunately, this approach is not in the hands of women. To avoid part-time traps, to live a hint of work-life balance and not to suffer from constant energy deficiency, I advocate here for the creation of a kind of large family system, consisting of partners, grandparents, private networks of mothers, service providers as well as daycare and school care. The argument of the solely blissful upbringing by women is a relatively recent product of our society. In the bourgeoisie, children were raised by nannies or lived in large families where siblings, grandparents, aunts, and uncles alternately took care of the provision and care of the children. This construct has dissolved in the last century. What speaks against reviving this system under different conditions?

The thesis that supermoms automatically produce superkids, I consider presumptuous, exaggerated, and not at all sustainable on a professional level. As with the presence question in companies, the same applies here:

> A present mother does not necessarily mean excellent upbringing, just as long-working executives do not automatically achieve good work quality.

We forget too quickly a differentiated view on both topics. Many men, but also women, make it too easy for themselves with unreflected platitudes that are simply parroted because this mindset is mainstream. And as we know, the mainstream is always right, isn't it?

> "Every person, men and women alike, should have the opportunity and strive beyond learned patterns to make life decisions freely, independent of societal role pressure and role understanding. I wish for us women that each of us recognizes what her wishes and needs are, where her boundaries lie and also when she puts herself in dependence, be it emotional or financial. Since women—like many men—take on several roles and responsibilities simultaneously in their professional and family lives, self-esteem is essential, because otherwise we easily move in a spiral of the

feeling of not being enough. With this realization, change processes can begin. It is then a conscious decision to change something, and in my eyes, that is where self-empowerment lies."
Michaela Kay, Consultant and Board Member.

5.5 Women and Their Side Stages: Girlfriend, Mother, Mother-in-law, and Network Partners

"Without family and friends, one lacks the wings in life." This quote comes from the UNESCO citizen dialogue from 2015. Most people in Germany do not live as singles, but in a partnership. Marriage is still the model that today's youth aspire to as a way of life. It is understood as a safety net against the "hostile" outside world. But it is not. We are often dealing here with dreams and wishful thinking. The realities, however, paint a different picture of marriage and family: every fourth woman is affected by domestic violence. The psychological abnormalities of children have increased during the Corona pandemic, but were also increasing beforehand. As a rule, the abnormalities of children originate in the family—unless they are genetically determined developmental disorders or other disease patterns. The perfect family does not exist, neither in Germany nor elsewhere.

The Phenomenon of Soft Violence
Behind abnormalities, physical or sexualized violence is often suspected. But there is a gray area, whose violence comes disguised. In the following chapters, I address the phenomenon of soft violence in the corporate context. It originates in the family of origin and takes its course from birth into professional life. Soft because no one suffers physical harm, the aggressions are not immediately recognized as aggressions or are often packaged as a gift, with the motto: "I only mean well for you". The story of the Trojan Horse would be an appropriate image at this point.

5 The Balancing Act between Partnership, Motherhood, and Career

The fact that women have no strength, energy, and desire for a career is also due to the fact that they receive imaginary stop signs from their environment—usually nicely packaged, but behind the official messages are unspoken signals, also in the form of facial expressions and gestures, that evoke feelings of guilt in women. The family of origin, in-laws, or girlfriends play a not to be underestimated role here. Women often do not really understand these messages because they interpret them as well-intentioned and do not grasp the actual meaning behind them.

"Child, I only want the best for you, you will overwork yourself if you increase your position. How do you want to manage two children and your job?" A seemingly well-intentioned objection, but the truth behind such statements is different. Often, one's own needs are diametrically opposed to the wishes of the daughter or girlfriend. One of the biggest taboos is the competition between mother and daughter. While the daughter begins to bloom, with a dream figure and wrinkle-free as well as all academic possibilities and potential employers who fight for top-educated men and women, the mother fades. With wrinkles, in menopause, divorced or unhappy in a partnership, some mothers find it difficult to support their daughters positively. It could happen that the daughters are actually doing better than they are. Do the sentences quoted at the beginning sound violent? No, not really, rather caring. But they are not. Depending on the situation, occasion, tone of voice, and body language, jealousy and envy are hidden behind this sentence. And possibly even the fear that the daughter will take care of neither the children nor the mother. To the image of the raven mother is added the ungrateful daughter, who prefers to make a career rather than provide elder care. This approach of the environment causes women immense feelings of guilt. As a result, they steer into a professional dead end, namely the career stop due to part-time position or/and the renunciation of a leadership position.

By the way, anyone who believes that women are always honest with each other and support each other in problems, advise each other or mediate jobs in women's networks, can be mistaken. Jealousy and envy also prevail here—with the difference that some women in networks hide behind roles in which they stage themselves. Honest and open communication with the aim of mutually supporting each other is rare.

> "I experience that this is changing. The proportion of those who open up to honest communication is growing—probably with age and experiences (disappointments), also and especially in top management. If you have already established a protected space, it is easy to use it. So I stick to the plea for networks!"
> Daniela Mündler, founder and managing director.

It follows that the career enemy is not only found in companies or within the couple relationship, but also in the family or private environment. Why is this? It is also about asserting one's own interests among women, for example by not really supporting the daughter or leaving the network partner in the lurch when she is looking for a job. In addition to jealousy and envy, other reasons are a distribution struggle for still few leadership positions for women or the identification with the male value system.

The large family system mentioned at the beginning will only work if women either have the luck to have people in their environment who actively and benevolently support them, or they have to actively look for such people.

Women as the extended arm of the patriarchy often make the career path even harder for women than it would have to be. They do not really solidarize, even if they pretend to do so. They organize themselves in women's networks, but do not support each other sufficiently here.

> "I wish for women who stand up for each other and together, who joyfully hatch plans for their advancement and develop strategies to cleverly and wittily parry attacks—be it privately or at work. In the sense of: One for all and all for one!"
> Doris Manthei, systemic family therapist and business coach.

We return to the thesis that women often do not know about their power, not even about the power in the collective. And if they do know, they are afraid to use it. Why? Because they have to reckon with the soft violent reaction of a system: If a woman in the company, for example, openly opposed the appointment of a man to a board position or if she openly branded experienced mobbing by superiors, she would become uncomfortable—attempts would be made to get rid of her with soft violence.

Let's now assume that women sent their men to the kitchen and took over the company management, this would mean for women to step out of their comfort zone and go to the "front" themselves. And this is associated with fears. In addition to fears of failure and the worry of not being able to reconcile the demands of the job with the needs of the family, there is also the fear of having to sacrifice one's own values. Because leadership positions entail no longer being able to be *Everybody's Darling* and having to tackle hot issues: It is necessary to speak plainly, conduct tough negotiations and sometimes dismiss people. But women generally have a need for harmony, which acts as compensation for a subtly violent system. But a company cannot be run with harmony alone. Those who take on powerful positions must commit to using this power for the company's goals—even if that means occasionally getting their hands dirty. This shakes women's self-image because their values are affected. To put the regime of role assignments *ad acta* also means dealing with one's own value compass and the values of the company as well as the divergences to the value system of patriarchally shaped structures and looking for sustainable solutions.

> To claim rights in company management or in the private environment, it requires brave women who are not afraid of losing their job, and above all, are not afraid of aggressive backlash. And this is best done in the community, in solidarity with other women.

Where is the way out of the regime of role assignments?

So how can women free themselves from the fear spiral of a violent system or partner, especially against the background of soft violence? Does this mean: Out of adaptation and into action? So out of the regime of role assignments?

"Become braver!" is a weak answer, because courage is something that has to be trained if it is not genetically determined or could not be developed in socialization.

I have two answers to this: Rights can be better enforced collectively, in the community, and enforcement requires suitable tools—strategies that women can apply at the moment of counter-reaction. In other words: They need a toolbox for handling role assignments.

Let's start with the collective, I'll get to the toolbox later. In Germany, there are numerous women's networks—in companies, on a club basis, on a political and private level. These networks initially serve for exchange, mutual support or as a job and business initiation platform.

> "Instead of lamenting the status quo and all injustices, the collected attention should rather be on personal development. It requires a good self-understanding for participation in economic life and mutual support beyond the thinking of scarcity ('there can be more than just one (woman)'). Then results will show much faster. Because energy follows attention, and it should always be on the solution, the goal, rather than on the problem."
> Dr. Ursula Koehler, systemic coach and expert for self-empowerment.

Often these networks slip into another corner: into that of the coffee chat hour, the self-staging stage or even into small battlefields, each against each. One cannot necessarily speak of a collective here. It is rather a union of women who hope to secure each other and generate well-being—and of women who disturb the well-being because they have other intentions. There are also women who want to draw more benefit from the networks than they are willing to give. They take everything and give nothing. Or women who manage women's networks on behalf of companies in order to write the topic of diversity on the company's flags. This leads to tensions and conflicts. Women's networks deal more with personal sensitivities and handle projects very superficially rather than with actual actions that should have a common goal: to help each individual member of this group to more status, income, power, job or contract. These networks lose sight of their goal or do not really have a goal.

5 The Balancing Act between Partnership, Motherhood, and Career

"In our economic world, men's networks have naturally emerged and are part of the working culture. Women's networks, in this respect, have the greatest need to catch up and women have to organize themselves specifically due to the male dominance in the working world to build networks. Probably women's networks today do not yet deliver what women hope for, namely to support equal participation, because they cannot develop sufficient strength when viewed in isolation. One reason is the complexity of the necessary change processes, including the leadership culture and orientation of the companies. Women also feel this in their networks and are perhaps more powerless than they would like, but at least they feel seen and supported by other women through the network, which strengthens them."
Michaela Kay, consultant and board member.

> Women have not yet noticed that they could undermine companies collectively.

Have you ever considered what would happen if women boycotted the purchase of various products whose manufacturers have no women on the board? Especially companies whose target group of buyers are women? They would soon be insolvent. Another scenario: A group of department heads and team leaders join together to demand more women at the management level. Do you think a demand from 100 women in the company can simply be ignored?

Such an uprising is unimaginable in Germany, even the protest movement #metoo would not be possible here. Because in this country—and this brings us back to the soft violence in companies—the isolation of women serves the system, it is intended. And women find it difficult to act collectively because they are entering taboo zones: out of adaptation and into power. Unimaginable. So they remain obedient and well-behaved.

And then their career path begins, after the stages of family of origin, puberty, partner choice, educated and ambitious, no children or already a mother. And here the next Trojan horse is saddled. Because young women think the corporate world is waiting for them. Factually correct in times of skills shortage—but only up to middle management, then it's over. With the exception of those women who are needed because of the quota or who have "fought their way through" in the companies.

Literature

Brandt, Marianne; Manthei, Doris; Lackner, Martina; Pamminger, Edith: Side-by-Side-Studie, 2020

Süddeutsche Zeitung (22. Oktober 2013): Der Sadist unter uns. https://www.sueddeutsche.de/wissen/psychologie-der-sadist-unter-uns-1.1799935. Zugegriffen: 7. September 2021

Bode, Sabine, Kriegsspuren. Die deutsche Krankheit German Angst, Klett-Cotta, Stuttgart, 2016

6

Leadership in Conflict—Discrepancy between Desire and Reality

Abstract Women want to lead, but differently than men. They usually have a higher value system and are disgusted by the microaggressions of male decision-makers. They disappear, go on parental leave, then return part-time and run the department as a secret boss in the background. In this way, they do not have to take on great responsibility, the fear of failing or falling short remains small.

The good news first: Career-minded women have a claim to leadership and would not want to give up their careers in favor of family work. The less good news: Most women do not want to lead (or have to lead) the way they are supposed to. There is a large discrepancy between the high value ideals of women, how they wish to lead, and what they experience in leadership. The following explanations on corporate structures and forms of leadership are taken from the Side-by-Side study (Brandt et al. 2020):

Women are seismographs with fatal consequences
With seismographic sensitivity, women experience an—often underground—authoritarian leadership scenario in which there is enormous

pressure to deny and conform. Instead of investigating the backgrounds for this and actively steering their own careers with these insights, they react with insecurity, nagging self-criticism, and idealism.

Especially young women, who are still at the beginning of their careers and have so far had little experience with subtly aggressive leadership styles, find themselves under great pressure. They are particularly susceptible to unjustified criticism and undermining messages from superiors because they have not yet been able to discover, try out, or further develop their own leadership in practice.

One of the biggest traps for these women is that they are too impressed by the assessments of their superiors. They do not recognize the deeper motives of their leader and take derogatory remarks about their behavior and their development opportunities at face value. On a psychological level, a fatal behavioral mechanism sets in, in which they unreflectively obey the defining power of the superior and obediently join the long line of supposedly more capable (mostly male) colleagues.

> What women often do not perceive are the more or less hidden resistances of superiors who hinder female employees in their progress. Existential fears and needs on the inner psychological level drive a large number of leaders to dysfunctional behaviors towards women.

"I should wait until I am asked. He also had to wait."
A participant of the Side-by-Side study 2020.

The consequence: Women apply for mentoring and women's advancement programs, want to participate in as many workshops and seminars as possible, but withdraw applications for (lowest) leadership positions when they are told that they do not bring practical experience, and show too little proactivity compared to their male colleagues.

> To put it bluntly: Instead of demanding leadership tasks, women let themselves be put on hold and stay there too long, some even for many years.

Women's advancement is based on a psychological twist

Women with several years of professional experience have a clearer view of the sometimes systematic career blockades in corporate culture. They often view internal women's advancement programs as a token action—the selection criteria often seem arbitrary and subjective to them. After going through the program, they do not progress, mentors are suddenly no longer approachable. When asked, they receive evasive or no answer.

> "The goal of the program is to say, we have a women's advancement program."
> A participant of the Side-by-Side study 2020.

Psychologically speaking, the programs represent a twist: They address a need for promotion in women due to a lack. But the lack, which is located on the women's side, is primarily a lack of sovereignty in male-dominated leadership ranks, caused by the defining power of a company-internal system that dictates how leadership should be. And these women are supposed to be educated and trained as leaders in the doctrine of a male-dominated leadership habitus. The lack is based on the attribution of a company that considers women to be deficient. From the good intention to strengthen women, the fatal signal results: Women are deficient, therefore they must be promoted. This leads to a supposed lack being structurally established even more strongly in the company, both in the perception of male colleagues and leaders and in the women themselves.

If we want to speak of a lack in women in this context, then it is a lack of unfolded power. In the female personality structure, there is a power vacuum with the exception of the power they exercise in the family context. However, this is rarely recognized as power and the strategies applied cannot be transferred 1:1 to the professional context. These require an adjustment. The power vacuum is based on a corresponding socialization process and the societal evaluation of power—especially that power exercised by women. The foundation for this is already laid in upbringing. To assert themselves, girls and women need power that must already be anchored in the personality. But this is not one of the female attributes of role attributions. Rather, I dare to claim, there is an internalized prohibition in our society for the female sex to grasp for power and thus develop their own power. Own power is not developed openly, but in a private context, so that it is usually not defined as power by the environment. The fact is: Men and women need power to lead a company. Now you might object: Power is obtained through positions. But how are women supposed to gain power if they don't get into these positions?

> Power is not acquired only through holding a leadership position. To get there, existing inner power is needed. If women want top positions, it is necessary to develop an awareness and an attitude for their own power.

It is to be hoped that in times of shortage of skilled and managerial staff—unfortunately born out of necessity—this lack issue will disappear and promotion programs will be launched that are more holistic, aimed at both genders. Simply because companies can no longer afford to do without women.

6.1 High demand and blind spot—this is how women lead

Women have excessive demands on themselves and their leadership style. This phenomenon is evident regardless of age, personality structure, and leadership experience. Women want to do particularly well, usually better than their superiors, under whom they have sometimes suffered greatly.

Nevertheless, there are also many women who act as leaders like the extended arm of the patriarchy because they copy the subtly violent style of patriarchal leadership: They, like their male colleagues, bring employees to obedience with control, disrespect, and microaggressions.

However, the more aggressive and unfair a leadership style appears in the company, the more the majority of women strive to lead as value-oriented, fair play, and with the highest quality standards as possible.

They develop ideal notions that are not sustainable in the long run and also rob them of a lot of energy in their daily work.

Some women, however, go "underground", lead indirectly, or reject leadership altogether. I also see this as a psychological consequence of dysfunctional power-helplessness structures that affect women's readiness and ability to lead.

The price women pay is not only difficult conditions for their own advancement but also the denial of feelings and needs. This makes women vulnerable and allows their talents and their power to shape to unfold only in a reduced form.

Why do women allow this?
This behavior can be explained by an unconscious need for regulation that prompts women to want to counterbalance the prevailing dysfunctional behaviors and norms in the company. Nevertheless, women lack a clear view of the actual power structures in the company. They urgently need this in order to be able to recognize where opportunities for change in the company end and violent structures begin.

I consider this blind spot to be an unconscious avoidance strategy, an indication of existential stress. In this respect, women behave in a systemically adapted manner and reflect with their need for regulation the actual dilemma, namely the negative effect of a dysfunctional leadership culture in the company itself.

Many women clearly reject hierarchical leadership based on principles of obedience and control. They place high demands on themselves and indirectly also on all levels of leadership in the company. Their ambition to achieve the best possible results is very pronounced. They want to lead in a value- and fact-oriented way. Morally integral action is on their side.

> Women strive for team spirit, an open, trusting relationship, and changing leadership constellations, always oriented towards the competence of the individuals and not their status.

Women want to lead in a consensus-oriented way and to involve as many employees as possible from their department or team. They are ready to take on a role model function through work commitment and integrity. And they advocate for a constructive error culture in which employees no longer have to hide behind excuses and avoidance strategies.

> Female leaders assume that people prefer to work in open and supportive systems where everyone can live out and contribute their abilities. They do not consider that this offered freedom can also trigger existential fears in people.

Especially people with low self-esteem and lack of ego strength feel more comfortable in work systems where they follow instructions or give instructions than in self-determined work structures. Authoritarian and hierarchically structured systems give them support. Through obedient and adapted behavior, such people hope for security. From a psychological point of view, this is a kind of follower phenomenon, which seems to be widespread in Germany and can be explained by the covert effects of transgenerational transmission.

Young people, both men and women, are increasingly seeking employment relationships that can be designed to be flexible both spatially and temporally. They want a relationship with their superiors on an equal footing, not one shaped by hierarchies.

> "Because they are so used to it from their families, many young people consciously desire clear structures that demand little responsibility, assign them a clear framework for action, and thereby convey security—at least as long as they have not yet entered the family formation phase. After that, time becomes scarce and the desire for flexibility increases—and at the same time becomes more difficult, because they are moving in a traditional, narrow system that they unfortunately also consciously chose."
> Dr. Ursula Koehler, systemic coach and expert for self-empowerment.

6 Leadership in Conflict—Discrepancy between Desire and Reality

Only a few companies will openly admit that they prefer an authoritarian leadership culture based on personal power preservation. After all, a contemporary, positive image is required as a marketing strategy today, especially in times of staff shortages. The actual desire is tabooed. Similar to closed family systems, all members adhere to the unofficial, secret rules. Into this silent agreement, women now want to lead openly and even advertise for it, without realizing how "dangerous" their approach is, especially for themselves.

> "With increasing leadership responsibility, it's about completely different criteria. Women know little about the don'ts and dos in hierarchical systems. When they recognize them in all clarity, they are horrified. As a result, they either leave or become excellent system players, but with a catch—until they no longer have the desire and drop out."
> Marianne Brandt, coach and organizational developer.

Systems regulate themselves. This means that if a leadership style deviates too far from the prevailing one, it will be undermined and the removal of the corresponding leader will be initiated sooner or later. As a rule, all actors in the system contribute to this directly or indirectly—from the team level to the top management.

> "I am considered difficult, I am authentic and call things by their name. Therefore, I am kept out. Despite my high technical knowledge, I am sidelined."
> A participant of the Side-by-Side study 2020.

Finding supposedly objective occasions and proving mistakes to the corresponding superior is no problem in everyday work. The fall is arranged as incompetence or gross leadership error with interchangeable reasoning. The actual mistake of the female leaders, however, is: They have failed to submit to the prevailing power culture.

Women who have had this experience have been removed from the company and often do not initially strive for leadership tasks after this experience. In any case, this experienced downfall is a heavy blow to their own self-esteem. Even experienced female leaders cannot simply shake off these mostly humiliating experiences. For them too, the question disturbingly remains open as to what they actually did wrong with all their good intentions.

> "We would be further along if all women recognized their scope for action and filled it with the values they want to bring into the world. Conversely, nothing will change as long as women do not perceive their own power as scope for action, but recoil, especially in the face of the incompatibility of their own values with given structures. A patriarchal hierarchy, i.e. predominantly our current system, often results in control, abuse of power and conflict when power is exercised. The form of cooperation in which male and female parts are appropriately balanced and support each other is synarchy, the sharing of power, the responsible cooperation on an equal footing. This is, in my view, the future we are already moving towards. Without a new understanding and without the equal perception of power by women, there can be no change. The individual determines the collective and vice versa. In view of the existing patriarchal ancient imprints of our system, it requires a very big step from women with a lot of mutual, but also male support in the sense of cooperation."
> Michaela Kay, consultant and board member.

When self-esteem and identity concept start to falter It is a bitter pill when women realize that they are not making progress in the company with their leadership approach. What they experience are power and violence scenarios. A usually male and sometimes incompetent leader demonstrates his power and points to the prescribed path. Even if the woman's suggestions could advance the company, they play a subordinate role in this system. As a result, the woman submits powerlessly. While she relies on technical competence, the stronger man relies on power demonstration. This is fatal for women, as a toxic reaction takes place here: The male leader recognizes that she would be the better boss, and makes the woman pay for it through humiliation, ignorance, and degradation. Her self-esteem and identity concept wobble.

6.2 Covert or Secret Leadership

The majority of women opt against this quite strenuous and risky approach. Instead, some women lead covertly or secretly, quite powerfully and influentially.

6.2.1 The Secret Boss

Operating from the second row, these women lead their boss by making themselves indispensable, compensating for their superiors' deficits, and leaving no doubt about their loyalty to their superiors to third parties.

External status, even more money or recognition as a leadership personality, are not important to these women or they deny their relevance. They pursue a motive that is of higher value to them, namely to ensure maximum control over their own lives. This includes securing their work situation, creating additional free spaces, and actively steering this. And that's exactly what they demand: home office, flexible working hours, increasing or reducing hours according to personal planning. Their superiors make many things possible because they can rely on their employee to always get the "hot coals" out of the fire for them, discreetly behind the scenes and without damage to the superior. This is also part of the often tacitly agreed arrangement.

> "I could do my boss's job and he knows it."
> A participant in the Side-by-Side study 2020.

It goes without saying, even without psychological interpretation, that these are likely to be weak leaders, perhaps even technically incompetent leaders, who have made their existence dependent on the loyalty of their subordinates. In psychology, we speak of a stable dependency system—here with the special variant that the higher-ranking person is the lower-ranking person in the internal relationship. That is, the personal dominance and ego strength with the need to be able to control both private and professional processes lies with the employee. The superior, on the other hand, is in a situation of overload from a psychological point of view, which must be constantly denied. It is usually impossible for this type of personality to put an end to this state, as his self-esteem and also his standard of living depend on his leadership role.

6.2.2 Leading Pleasurably in Secret

Another variant of secret leadership is used by women with low leadership aspirations. Here too, it is about dependency situations in which the superior must necessarily build trust in his employees.

Longer absences, illness-related failures, overload with new tasks and projects can be the reason for women to take over the leadership from the background. In consultation with colleagues and in the sense of cooperative leadership, the work is organized and carried out with a corresponding positive boost in motivation for everyone.

The motives for this approach are clearly of an immaterial nature. Thus, the employees have long been longing for open and self-determined work, but cannot bring this work style due to the anxious-adaptive and controlling attitude of their superiors. Intrinsically motivated, all participants pitch in to accomplish the project or task as best as possible.

> "Without our boss, it was really fun and we were successful."
> A participant in the Side-by-Side study 2020.

6.3 The Denied Leadership Claim

In the case of the denied leadership claim, women do not acknowledge or admit to themselves that they aspire to leadership, or they have detailed explanations for why they cannot (or do not) take on leadership. These women appear agitated and also contradictory when asked about their professional career opportunities based on their special competencies.

In fact, they have a lot of leadership, they want to shape and also have power and influence. This group consists of women who come from violent families of origin. As much as they could in these great dependencies as a child and later as a teenager, they tried to resist the parental threats with a lot of fighting spirit and great courage.

6.4 Renouncing Leadership as a Protective Measure

I assume that some women who shy away from leadership responsibilities are traumatized by their childhood experiences and, in a way, recoil from their own high potential for aggression. In psychology, this is referred to as the internalization of parental aggression, which is extremely difficult for those affected to handle, especially in stressful situations. Thus, an eruptive outbreak in a business context would be tantamount to a disaster, so it is plausible that these women deny or relocate their leadership claim as a kind of "protective measure" to the private sphere.

> "The price is a certain joylessness, even in dealing with colleagues. I myself have also been aggressive."
> A participant of the Side-by-Side study 2020.

Losing or Hiding
Women and men lead differently. While women orient themselves towards values, team orientation, democratic principles, and optimal results, men, especially those of the older conservative leadership, rely on dominance. Unfortunately, the seemingly strong man is still trusted more with leadership competence in companies than a woman. This usually leads women only to middle management. They react to this dilemma differently: Some start to play a role and hide their true selves. They train behaviors they think would be well received in the male-dominated world. In the process, not only does their true self disappear, but the facade construction also consumes energy. They would need this energy to assert themselves. Their self is subsequently weakened. Others adapt through obedience and split off their emotions. Body language, voice, expression, and appearance demonstrate humble femininity. Existing aggressions are suppressed, negative experiences are swept under the rug. But

this makes them even more powerless: Anyone who radiates that they will not defend themselves is an easy victim.

The Wrong Strategy

Women are told they should become more visible. But visibility should not mean show, otherwise it appears untrustworthy. Women lose their authenticity through lack of or missing authentic behaviors, missing adequate reactions when they are attacked, and by denying their values, the enforcement of which they fail to achieve. Women with a high degree of adaptation and obedience not only destroy themselves because such processes are exhausting, but they also rely on the wrong strategy. Because at the top, a resilient and assertive self is required—anyone who does not have this will not last long here. Even if the quota has brought them to a position of power.

Blind Spot

Women who fail to analyze their male counterparts soberly, but rather have a clouded view of motives and patterns, tend to "fall for" superiors, colleagues, and partners. They cannot correctly interpret their signals and behaviors, harbor hopes that are not fulfilled, or are surprised and hurt when they are left in the rain by the male counterpart. Women often have a blind spot here.

> **What to Do?**
> - Learn to appreciate yourself.
> - Stop self-denial and become who you are—even if you are afraid of not finding a leadership job or suitable partner.
> - The danger of self-denial often already implies a victim status. Those who determine their own path gain power—also over themselves.

Literature

Brandt, Marianne; Manthei, Doris; Lackner, Martina; Pamminger, Edith: Side-by-Side-Studie, 2020

7
Power and Powerlessness: The Experienced Leadership

Abstract Women experience not only disrespect from their colleagues in companies. In addition to sexism, there is also open or subtly aggressive behavior from managers towards them. The motto on the corporate battlefield is still all too often: keep women down and "soften" them.

Women who work in power-impotence systems are angry, very insecure, and injured women. Such conflicting emotions are considered in psychology as warning signs for openly or covertly acting power-impotence systems. As a rule, these are not isolated situations, but a widespread phenomenon in the German corporate landscape. The following statements come from participants of the Side-by-Side study (Brandt et al. 2020). Their statements show the emotional dimension of the everyday experience. The seemingly harmless "business as usual" in its actual, sometimes grotesque effect, cannot be better described by experts than with the statements of these women:

7.1 And Daily Greet Dogma, Dominance and Dismantling

Lack of empathy and obedience at any cost

- "I made a mistake. I should also say in the end that I will never do it again."
- "My boss says: I give instructions, I make decisions, I give orders, people dance to my tune."
- "Staff is just a number and that's it."
- "It does something to women when they are constantly bashed."
- "They would have grilled me already in the application process."
- "In the past, I didn't care what position a person held. Today, I am more afraid."

Incompetent leadership and denied fear

- "You only get to the top if you are incompetent."
- "He didn't want to hire me as an intern because I could blow up his team."
- "I was told: I should have understanding for this boss because he was kicked out by his wife two years ago."
- "With incompetence, you get further and that annoys me. I find it terrible!"
- "My mentor reflected to me that my superior is afraid of me. He wanted to keep me small."

Dusty leadership structures and outdated snobbery

- "I am young and dynamic and want to live HR more modernly; instead old smoky, staid corporations."
- "Leading by presence is easier than by goals. You can do that with a time clock, you don't even need three brain cells for that."

7 Power and Powerlessness: The Experienced Leadership

- "Initially, my employees had reservations about me as a female boss. Now that I have taken over another department, they don't know if they can still cope with the old leadership style."
- "Men don't see why they should submit to me."
- "You are a woman, you won't get any further anyway."
- "I acted on an equal footing, and he didn't like that because I expressed my opinion and put myself on their level."
- "The intuitive reflex of male systems is: We do everything better and faster. People are replaced. That doesn't hold."
- "In industries or companies shaped by German engineering, the absence of a culture of error is systemic."
- "The old leadership has already positioned their protégés."
- "The goal of the board was to maintain the quota: 16% women in leadership positions. Yet we have over 50% women in the company."
- "He once asked me if I was from another planet. I said: I am on Earth, where are you?"

Opaque powerfully and in solidarity

- "In this company, performance doesn't count, but how you sell yourself."
- "Among men, there is a 'friendly competition', women are rather perceived as competition."
- "I was disappointed with the company policy that first covers and protects people from top to bottom and looks less at the factual content."
- "A woman in leadership positions then gets ahead if she gets along well with the men."
- "I believe it was a power game. And we were the means to an end, the sacrificial pawn."
- "I have not been able to recognize to this day according to which criteria they promote people."
- "Not the best ideas win, but the ideas of the one who has the best relationships."
- "I was told they know it's important to bring women into leadership. I don't know if it's a real belief or an intellectual intention."

Women who do not want to work under these conditions choose the way out of starting a family, so to speak the gentle exit from a conglomerate of career obstacles. They have children, disappear into parental leave and justify their career break with family needs. Motherhood becomes a justification for the exit scenario. In this process, the company is put to the test: Was it the right choice?

7.2 Career Break Motherhood?

The statements in this subchapter are taken from the Side-by-Side study (Brandt et al. 2020).

Women are increasingly interested in balancing career and motherhood. Career-minded women are far from overemphasizing motherhood. They know very well how important reliability and commitment are to their employer, and are willing to contribute to this. But one thing is also clear to them: They do not want to have to pretend as if they do not have children.

> Women put companies to the test: Women with and without children look very closely at how companies deal with the issue of motherhood. They notice what happens to colleagues returning from parental leave and how female career paths are represented up to the highest levels.

"They sidelined her. That shocked me a lot."
A participant of the Side-by-Side study 2020.

Performance-oriented mothers are upset and angry about the actions of companies. They are annoyed by the inflexibility and "old habits" of companies, their handling of mothers and unfair strategies to keep them away from the power centers. The number of companies criticized on this issue is significantly high.

Power games or fair play in the test

Women are not only concerned with how they assess their opportunities in the company to balance career and family, but they also test the honesty of the company and its executives, look for hidden power games and the integrity of their superiors. The company's value system is on trial.

Women's willingness to show loyalty and identify with the company depends significantly on how honest, transparent, and fair it is with this issue.

The good news: Companies have it in their own hands in which direction to turn the motivation screw—tightening with power games or loosening in fair play.

Recognizing power structures in the company

Some women have fine antennas and very good observational skills, with which they recognize what is really going on in the company. If those in leadership positions want to use women's motherhood to slow them down, the affected can become very uncomfortable—directly or subtly hidden: The strategies range from "Then I'll just stay at home!" to legal disputes.

> "When I told my CEO that I was expecting my third child, I could see how he mentally removed me from the leadership board and his succession. I knew then: I'm out. I told my husband that I can now call an employment lawyer. The employment relationship then also ended with a legal dispute."
> A participant of the Side-by-Side study 2020.

The behaviors experienced in companies that alienate women during pregnancy and after the birth of their child include, among others:

- the undermining, which already begins during pregnancy, through inappropriate remarks such as: "I don't trust you to do more than part-time work with a child";
- the manipulation after parental leave with the aim of persuading the woman to work part-time;

- the withdrawal of projects and tasks—instead, she receives jobs that no one wants to do upon her return from parental leave;
- the exclusion from the email distribution list in the final phase of a project, even though the woman is responsible for the project;
- the limiting of perspectives, through announcements like: "You are not at all suitable for leadership jobs";
- the transfer to another, less significant position, even though the previous work could have been done part-time with reasonable restructuring (for example, with the support of student workers);
- conducting business conversations in a purely male circle, the female colleague is only addressed as a mother;
- the shifting of meetings, which previously took place during the day, to the evening hours;
- the rejection of her suggestions for improving the personal work situation without a comprehensible reason;
- the ignoring of further training wishes;
- the absence of conversations about personal development.

Women react very sensitively to this kind of exclusion and devaluation, especially when the issues cannot be addressed and clarified on a factual level.

Companies with such an excluding habit will lose not only competent women with children in the short or long term, but also young women from their talent pools, because they can no longer imagine a future in this company due to such behaviors.

So much for motherhood as a career setback
Especially career-minded women are focused on work, want to advance professionally and have clear ideas about how this can work with children. They are willing to do their part, but also expect the company to adapt to their situation.

> Supervisors should not make the mistake of viewing motherhood as a problem of the employee or even thinking that she currently has no other professional perspectives.

If women believe that it is not a matter of basic company policy, but perceive their superiors as a hindrance, they look for internal transfer opportunities early on. Whether the company supports the desired change or continues to hold them back determines whether they will remain loyal to the company or leave. In the end, they stand by the employer who accommodates them in the work structures and at the same time offers serious career opportunities.

> "He probably thought: What does she want? She has two children and can't get anywhere else quickly."
> A participant in the Side-by-Side study 2020.

7.3 Backgrounds for the Devaluation of Mothers by Superiors

Even if most superiors might claim that the solutions, restrictions, and professional dead ends of women were (always) necessary and were made on a factual basis, these justifications are not believed by the women. To put it bluntly, women do not let themselves be "sold for stupid".

> "You didn't lose your brain when you had children!"
> A participant in the Side-by-Side study 2020.

What are the underlying reasons that lead superiors to devalue mothers, not accommodate them, or not consider them for leadership positions?

High need for security
Deviating from usual procedures and processes makes these superiors insecure. They are characterized by low flexibility and secure themselves through rather adapted, rule-compliant procedures. The fear of receiving criticism from their superiors makes them back down, so they do not communicate even good and easily implementable solutions. The leadership style is rather hesitant. There is an inner psychological insecurity among these leaders as to whether they are seen as full-fledged

and competent leadership by the employees. Avoidance is their primary strategy to maintain their own leadership position.

Exercising power through control
The availability of employees is enormously important for this superior—be it through time control or the scheduling of spontaneous meetings. Superiors with this need require presence and control over the status of work at all times as a safeguard of their own position. A certain unpredictability and rigidity emanate from this leadership style.

> "It does something to your self-esteem. They see themselves in this position, it gives them a kick."
> A participant in the Side-by-Side study 2020.

Such leaders do not want to be the plaything for others, so they reverse the signs. The presence and availability of their employees give them support and security.

This strategy often does not work with mothers. While mothers themselves are more flexible, they are no longer reliably available. This is experienced by the superior as a breach of loyalty—even if it is not. This superior rejects pragmatic solution suggestions from the employee because they do not provide him (or her) with inner psychological security. A fatal and frustrating situation for both sides, which cannot be sustained in the long run.

Self-esteem attack by successful mothers
Imagine, women can have (well-behaved) children and at the same time be successful up to top management levels. What does this mean for the performance of the man, who is usually backed by his wife at home and can concentrate more or less exclusively on his career? His performance seems diminished. Self-insecure leadership personalities therefore experience "high-flyer" women as an attack on their authority and right to exist.

A very unfortunate vicious circle arises when the woman in turn strives to show everyone that she is fully up to the task—despite children. Her intention is to create trust and reliability. She is not aware that she achieves exactly the opposite with it. Both are in a kind of inner psychological movie, but not the same one. While one movie is titled: "Trust me, I can handle my work, even though I am a mother", the other is titled: "Who am I if I am less?"

This conflict arises from rigid role assignments, which are increasingly being softened by women. This feeds into a great dilemma for men, as their right to exist is (almost exclusively) based on gainful employment and the status achieved (measured in title, money, number of employees, public reputation, etc.).

> In my view, men get into an inner psychological conflict when mothers are present at all levels of leadership. But the solution is not to keep them away.

Instead, I recommend men to expand their mindset—knowing that this could also be a pious wish. A conviction that says: "I am more than my job", is not or not pronounced. Nevertheless, it could be a (hidden) longing theme for men.

Successful Mothers Threaten Their Own Family Model

This topic concerns supervisors who follow the classic family and marriage model, where women work part-time, have little career ambition, or are not employed at all. Holding the status of the family's main breadwinner is very important to them. For these men, it can therefore be quite unsettling when a committed employee continues to pursue a full-time career despite having children, possibly becoming the main breadwinner of her family.

Tendencies to undermine these women and no longer consider them for further tasks are strongly pronounced in such supervisors. A mother committed to her job will have no opportunities for development with them.

In the background, these supervisors fear that their own wife might also strive for more independence. In terms of a countertransference, as the term from psychology goes, the employee is denied what they actually want to deny their wives.

"Why do we bring children into the world? My wife should take care of the childcare. Why should she work?"
A participant of the Side-by-Side study 2020 on statements made by her supervisor. Unfortunately, this phenomenon is not a dying model. As long as men are demanded to have a (too) high performance and commitment, their family support and a domestic wife are of central importance to them.

Women in Competition: What I Didn't Have, I Won't Grant You
Competition among women is a weighty issue, as it undermines female-specific support opportunities in a special way. It is particularly bitter when older female supervisors block the development opportunities of younger women, show disinterest, or show off talented employees in front of others.

Women are unsettled and partly also shocked by the harshness. The lack of support here may well be due to personal losses and injuries of their female superiors from the time of their career development and the fact that these could not be processed. In these cases, we speak of compensation strategies, which can also run unconsciously, to remain up to the professional demands. This armor of strength, built up over many years, can offer only moderate protection in situations where the hidden issue is reflected through the encounter in the outside world. Paving the way for young women is perceived as too painful internally. The alternative reaction is rejection and even attack. Facing these injuries would be a good chance to heal old wounds. At the same time, these experienced women could ensure that, in addition to the male-oriented career paths, female-appropriate career paths can also develop.

7.4 Lack of Personal Responsibility and Its Consequences

Women want child *and* career. But they often lose their way: When they become mothers, the bonding hormone oxytocin creates an emotional bond to the child. Added to this are their own and general ideas of what makes a "good" mother. Shifts also occur in the partnership:

Women often believe they are the only ones who know exactly what the offspring need and who can take care of them best, so they deny this competence to their partner. They thus assume a dominant role within the family system. At the same time, the man is under pressure to secure the family income in such a way that the accustomed standard of living is maintained.

In the job, the perspectives for the woman change through the birth of a child. So what happens? She increasingly focuses on the child, thereby nourishing her often low self-esteem. Young women usually do not yet understand the pitfalls of development from motherhood.

> As mothers, women often define themselves by the well-being of their family, not by their own well-being.

But when the partner reorients himself later in the midlife crisis and the children have become independent, a feeling of lack sets in. The previous life concept falls short. Now the topic of job and career gains importance again—either to fill the void or to fill the bank account. The perceived pain becomes the drive. However, a woman who has driven her own career from the beginning without a cooperative partner and a support system, loses many feathers: The woman has no time for herself, but performs a permanent split between career, child, man, household and extended family at the expense of her own strength. See also Sect. 5.3.2.

In both life paths, women do not take enough responsibility for themselves. Their life revolves too much around others, they do not take care of their own resources or needs—they are basically "powerless" when it comes to their own concerns. This powerlessness is to be understood as learned helplessness. Many women make themselves dependent on their partner within the family system on various levels—not only in terms of financial provision, but also in terms of everyday competencies. They leave certain fields to the man and do not try to develop skills here as well. This puts them partially in a helplessness that they only feel painfully when the partner no longer takes over these tasks.

> Women's self-esteem is still all too often attached to the care of their children and the associated recognition from the outside or to meeting all expectations perfectly.

Powerful in the Family System

The secret power of women lies in caring for the family. Through their role as mothers, they gain power over the family. This compensates them for the lack of power in the outside world—even if this power leaves much to be desired in terms of money, recognition, and prestige. However, it dissolves with the detachment process of the children.

Literature

Brandt, Marianne; Manthei, Doris; Lackner, Martina; Pamminger, Edith: Side-by-Side-Studie, 2020

8

Principles of Violence in German Companies

Abstract Principles of violence arise where people feel threatened. In companies, competent, high-performing, well-educated women pose a danger to male executives. The threat borders on the existential justification of men—in financial terms, but also in psychological terms. The identity of career men is largely fed by professional success, power, money, and status. Successful women destroy this hero principle. Not only because there are fewer jobs in top positions when women move up. But also, in the future, there will be hero*ines* who lead, save, or help companies to profit. What kind of man am I if a woman is just as good as I am?

8.1 Our Collective Heritage

The essence of the power-impotence system in which we find ourselves is violence—even if it is often not recognizable at first glance. To put it bluntly: German leadership culture, especially in conservative sectors, still has the habitus of a violent system. What is meant here is soft and subtle violence, which demands obedience and adaptation from women and men. Soft, because it has no physical character, after all, there is no beating in German offices, and subtle, because the strategies and behaviors applied are not recognized as violence. These trivialized violence structures are at the center of transgenerational transmissions (cf. Sect. 2.1). They are also an expression of socialization and imprinting by beliefs in the family of origin.

Unconsciously, depending on the industry and company, a war scenario is reenacted in Germany, in which the division into perpetrators and victims, winners and losers increases, hollows us out and impoverishes us immaterially. Many more companies could have long since embarked on the path of implementing heterogeneous, as gender-parity as possible, management levels, allowing more effective working models, actually introducing equal pay for men and women, and developing trust in employees—instead of building control systems and power-impotence structures.

But a deeply rooted fear, which is hardly comprehensible at the factual level, prevents these processes, under which women and men, albeit not in the same way, suffer with fatal consequences (source: Side-by-Side study, Brandt et al. 2020).

> "Any action that springs from fear, especially in an unconscious repressive reaction to a fear, can in my eyes not have a positive sustainable effect or change. Everything that fuels our fear manipulates people into trying to protect themselves, closing themselves off, excluding themselves or others, and clinging to supposed security. And we react collectively more with impotence and rigid adherence to a once established survival strategy. Deep-seated fears, here in Germany for example noticeable war traumas that run through families, were and are as visible as perhaps not since the Cold War. On the other hand, I also see a more differentiated and deeper perception of this. Realization is always the first step for a change."
> Michaela Kay, consultant and board member.

8.2 The Fear of Leadership of Competent Women

The following remarks are largely taken from the Side-by-Side study (Brandt et al. 2020).

A deep-seated existential fear is the reason why women are systematically undermined, spin endless loops in women's promotion programs, and are regularly not nominated for higher tasks.

> "It is existential fear, but also an unconscious entanglement (let) in secondary battlefields such as women's promotion programs, mentorings with coffee trip character, women's project groups—everything where a separation between the sexes continues to be created, cannot work sustainably. Instead of reacting, it is necessary to build and shape a new path from within oneself."
> Dr. Ursula Koehler, systemic coach and expert for self-empowerment.

Devaluing women, considering them not good enough, making demands with messages like "Become active" or "You have to wait your turn with us!" that they cannot fulfill, or pushing mothers into uninteresting jobs, are indications of a high need for security of the leadership for their own survival in the system.

Promoting women in the company ultimately means for men to give up some of their power—which means attacking the right to exist of male superiors and colleagues at the psychological level. Career-ambitious women are thus a permanent threat in everyday work. The fear of job and power loss triggers communication strategies that are basically nothing more than manipulation strategies. Losing to a woman or having to be led by her is a great disgrace for these men. This triggers feelings of shame and must therefore be prevented.

> Women are undermined, softened, and manipulated at the communicative level, verbally and non-verbally, until they give up, go into refusal, or renounce leadership positions—and disappear into the apparent comfort zone of the affluent family. All these are signs of a "defensive war" against competent women. The violence is permanently present in the system, but at the same time well camouflaged.

"Unfortunately, this is only too true. My husband definitely recognized this several times before me, even without knowing the people and based only on my reports. Each time, I took significantly longer to see it and pull the plug to seek my fortune elsewhere."
Dr. Angelika Weinländer-Mölders, chemist, manager and co-editor of *Side by Side—Men at the Side of Successful Women*.

When women are asked about their experiences of subtle violence in companies, they tend to intellectualize and trivialize the descriptions of the (every)day aggressions in the office. Their own justified aggression as a response to violent behaviors is suppressed. Their experiences and observations are assigned to usual categories: "business as usual" or "that's just the way it is". This means, women deny and suppress their feelings and adapt to the prevailing language and opinion habitus.

I see in this behavior another indication that the tabooing of a subliminally frightening topic is taking place at the inner psychological level.

8.3 The Consequence: Women Do Not Reach Their Full Power

The following explanations are predominantly taken from the Side-by-Side study (Brandt et al. 2020).

Those who cannot clearly perceive what is actually effective in the corporate system, and suppress feelings, cannot activate their strategies for resistance and distancing or demarcation. If aggression is not perceived as aggression, no adequate behavior can develop as a consequence. In psychology, we speak of bound energy. Far too many women remain at the assigned level instead of actively taking care of their careers due to this binding.

Reduction of Self-Esteem and Ego Strength
This very mechanism of standing still, which works in many women, is career killer No. 1: Women deny their feelings. They persist (for too long) in violent, blocking structures. They systematically work in and on the system, with the consequence of being less and less sure of their own self-esteem and ego strength. The fact that they no longer see themselves as suitable for leadership tasks over time can be a fatal result of this degradation process.

In my estimation, the male-dominated system wants to achieve exactly this. However, I do not consider this intention to be a basic malevolence, but an existentially important safeguarding mechanism triggered by hidden fears and feelings of threat.

8.4 Women's Blind Spots as an Indication of Fear-Violence Spirals

The following explanations are predominantly taken from the Side-by-Side study (Brandt et al. 2020).

"No Connection Under This Number"
One insight that particularly shocks me is that women do not recognize the threat they trigger in the system. Career-ambitious women are consistently excellently educated, multilingual, have doctorates with long stays abroad, bring leadership, are reflective, ready for a healthy error culture, and yet do not see themselves as serious and frightening competition to superiors and colleagues.

This does not seem to fit into women's self-image and is therefore not related to what is actually experienced, a kind of "no-connection-under-this-number" phenomenon. From my point of view, this phenomenon shows a fear-driven, adapted behavioral strategy in the face of the underlying aggression they experience in everyday work. If you will, it is an attempt at an unconscious gesture of submission to violence.

I assume that women intuitively perceive fears and developing threat scenarios at the unconscious level and react fearfully to them in turn. In systemic psychology, we speak of fear-violence spirals, which can hardly be perceived as such in the work context.

> The tip of the iceberg becomes visible in German companies when escalations occur. Even in these cases, one must expect that many people in the system are ready to put these into a context of "business as usual" even in the event of severe collisions.

"Many companies like to forget that information, such as certain groups of people being treated worse, spreads on the internet. Before accepting a job, one informs oneself and such bad information not only deters female applicants."
Theresa Nerz, Board Member/Social Media Manager.

Women are well advised to give up the strategy of the three wise monkeys—see nothing, hear nothing, say nothing. Instead, they should deal with the phenomenon that men are afraid of them, even if this is denied and hidden behind a power habitus.

8.5 Burying the Hatchet

The following remarks are predominantly taken from the Side-by-Side study (Brandt et al. 2020).

Firstly, we must understand that many decision-makers and employees who regulate economic life have deep-seated existential fears, which are not trivial. In my view, it would be completely unrealistic to expect them to change structures that bring women into leadership. After all, this would psychologically equate to a "harakiri act".

Therefore, the first important step was to introduce a women's quota.

"The question is: How well does the women's quota work? Up to which management level does it apply, is it desired?"
Dr. Ursula Koehler, systemic coach and expert in self-empowerment.

A quota alone is not a sustainable solution to end a "defensive war". Despite all the losses that would mean less or no career for men, a positive balance is needed. We need a perspective that could have a liberating effect. This way, men could deal with the fact that they are more than just their job. They could broaden their life plans, free themselves from the burden of being the (sole) breadwinner in the family, and derive their self-worth more from their personality than from being defined by hierarchy levels, bonuses, and the size of their company car.

The decision-makers in the company have a duty
Violent structures cannot be changed with a few nicely formulated rules of conduct in company agreements and corporate principles. Violent structures must be unmasked in daily actions and named as such. Decision-makers must have the courage to look in the mirror and take responsibility for their own behavior. And then it is their task to ensure that effective measures are taken in the company.

It must be clear to all employees that violence in their company will not be tolerated.

This is a difficult task, especially because particularly hierarchical structures more or less consciously promote a culture of fear, which precisely aims to adapt and secure one's own position. Therefore, especially managers must question themselves and work on themselves.

"We need more female-influenced qualities in leadership, regardless of gender, and a more balanced distribution of power to sustainably shape change processes. Whoever is given power is not only responsible for certain tasks, but—like every human being—is challenged to take responsibility for themselves and to be able to reflect where, for example, certain external demands or the behavior of others trigger their own injuries or fears. We react with defense and reaction when we are afraid or feel attacked. In particular, we often become dominant. Coupled with power or a leadership position, this easily becomes a form of power that we fear or condemn. Power in this form then also does not serve the leadership role and can even be abusive. In addition to other qualities, leadership therefore primarily needs empathy, an awareness of one's own experiences, and the willingness to develop oneself."

Michaela Kay, consultant and board member.

8.6 The Brake Block Fear

I have already hinted that women need strategies and tools to confidently confront an aggressor in the moment of aggression—regardless of whether it is a partner, a superior, or a colleague. These strategies are lacking because they are neither learned nor trained. Women have grown up in patterns of fear and carry a past within them. Dealing with aggression and violence is like a blank white sheet of paper for them.

Violence has been a constant companion of women for thousands of years, in private as well as in professional life. But it does not always occur openly, but much more often in secret or in such a way that it is not initially recognized as violence. Signs of a violent society include sexism, exclusion from leadership positions and training measures, humiliation and belittlement, and much more—behaviors that are cemented by men and even supported by women.

Women unconsciously react to possible violence scenarios: In order not to upset their own partnership when they pursue their career, they do not negotiate with their partner, but exhaust themselves trying to juggle job and family. There are no laurels for this. Rather, they sometimes experience that their boss claims the work they have done as his own and promotes a male colleague. In other words: Women allow themselves to be exploited and shy away from confrontation because they are afraid. Either they perceive this fear directly or they harbor it as an uneasy feeling. Only a few women are fearless. The result: There is no self-understanding of women having a right to a career, to self-development and needs. They define themselves through others, rarely through themselves.

Equality cannot be achieved solely through laws and diversity efforts. Over archaic principles, a culture of democracy, freedom, and equality has developed over the millennia, and most recently, the equality of the sexes in leadership positions. But this is a cultural, not a biological development. Therefore, men still test women at the first encounter: What is possible with this woman? Is she an object of desire? Or is she taking my job away? This program runs partly consciously, partly unconsciously. Any woman who does not resist this check, but signals submission, dependence, or obedience through rhetoric, gestures, facial expressions, and body language, has already lost. Women are always on trial. Even if regulations and laws demand equality, male emotions and attitudes remain unaffected. Because men also have fear, namely the fear of competent women. The fear that they will be overtaken professionally, their chances of a career will dwindle, their performance will be worse compared to highly trained women. Male competition, the competition with men and their lust for power accompany women in their job as well as in private life.

> **What needs to be done?**
> - Realize that your environment, both private and professional, also always pursues its own interests. Here nicely packaged traps await when it comes to doing something without payment or selflessly to the point of self-sacrifice so that others can benefit. Don't let yourself be softened, belittled or kept small, guilt-tripped or deluded with lofty ideals.
> - Stop believing that you are not good enough, following false beliefs, being undereducated or a bad mother! Instead, start trusting your gut feeling.
> - Stop avoiding, enduring or reinterpreting your problems!
> - You only gain power over violent situations or people if you leave the situation, i.e. quit the job, get transferred, put your partner or even your closest family to the test—and draw consequences.
> - Get into action! Women are more interested in sharing their problems than solving them. If you want power, you have to learn to address unpleasant situations or people, to negotiate, to set conditions, to confront or even to separate. This needs to be learned!

Literature

Brandt, Marianne; Manthei, Doris; Lackner, Martina; Pamminger, Edith: Side-by-Side-Studie, 2020

9

Tools and Strategies for Dealing with Powerfully Aggressive People

Abstract Power-impotence spirals are relationship patterns that women experience more or less daily. However, they sometimes no longer perceive them as a spiral in which a powerful man drives them into the position of the powerless. For many women, such relationship patterns are rather everyday life, they are used to it. The toolbox of this chapter serves to exit such spirals.

9.1 How Do I Extricate Myself from Power-Impotence Relationships?

I ask this question because most women have enormous difficulties in either completely dissolving ties, i.e., bringing about a separation or breaking away from their employer, or at least distancing themselves emotionally from powerfully aggressive people.

Women typically have a high value and moral system, are extremely loyal, take responsibility for child, family, and job, and live in the hope that their relationship with their boss, partner, or even with powerful women will improve someday. They believe in the insight of the other person, in their own ability to change the other person if they just persist long enough. Women have an enormous capacity for suffering or they tend to view life through rose-colored glasses, or they hope that the proof of love will come in the form of a promotion or as attention from their partner. Do you remember the image of the prince riding up? The princess hopes for redemption and eternal happiness.

The fixation on the male counterpart
When I speak of dissolving bonds here, I primarily mean the dissolution of the relationship on an emotional level, which is followed by the detachment on a factual level. By factual, I mean, for example, a termination, divorce, dissolution of the household, job search. When we go into the emotional area, which is long before the decision to change, the detachment from the relationship becomes more intricate and complex because many women live and work in a fixation on the male counterpart. And not only because many bosses are men or most women have love relationships with men, but because women feel they would not be complete without a man. They believe they could not manage their lives without a strong partner at their side—here I do not primarily mean the financial aspect, but the emotional one. It is a kind of existential fear, an archaic feeling that a man ensures their own survival.

And so women encounter powerful men who play out their power in the patriarchal system of our society when they have the opportunity and weapons to do so. Their weapons range from verbal threats to actual use of weapons. I repeat myself here: Power in its negative form will strive to take possession of someone, among others, these are women. In this construct, women are also joined by the fear of male weapons and violence. That means: Women look for strong men to lean on and who give them security. But these very men may lead them to ruin: The power will take possession of these women. For women, the factor of the child is an additional complication. If we assume an archaic principle here, it is the man's task from the women's point of view to ensure not only the survival of his wife but also that of his children.

> **What can you do?**
>
> Why not treat yourself to a systemic structural setup on the topic of power and impotence—then you will get an idea of the forces at work and input for solution approaches.
> Marianne Brandt, coach and organizational developer.

The desire for a strong man

This constellation arises because women are weakened both physiologically and psychologically: due to pregnancy, childbirth, and then raising children. They are thus not only financially undersupplied and therefore dependent, but also energetically undersupplied and in need of protection, which is misinterpreted by women and exploited by men.

Women can theoretically take care of themselves, they do not really need the financial support of their partner. A common child is not solely their responsibility, but that of a pair of parents. This means: The protection that women really need is only temporary—namely for the time they need to recover after giving birth. From this point on, a *couple* has a child, with parental duties for *both*. The archaic principle of survival assurance has become obsolete in 2023.

The call for the strong, dominant, assertive man is a phenomenon that can be observed not only in relation to women. Entire nations seek strong leaders from whom they hope for rescue and redemption. German history is a prime example of this. And the rescuers then lead the people into an actual struggle for survival. The end is known.

This phenomenon is explained to me by the fact that people are hardly able to take responsibility for themselves. They just think they do. The blame for crisis situations in their own lives, challenging life situations or problems in corporations is automatically sought outside, responsibility is shifted. And anyone who generally shifts responsibility also assumes that the rescue must lie outside. But rescue is linked to power and thus often enough to violence.

When children are involved, women's need for security increases, at the same time they submit even more to the "strong" man. Or they turn the game around: Some women use their children to secure a golden cage for themselves. At first, they do not realize that it is more cage than gold.

How exactly does the power-impotence spiral between men and women work?
Power-Impotence spirals are cemented by hierarchies, by status and qualification, by roles or by the level of income. However, they arise on an emotional level, in the relationship structure between the sexes. More precisely, they already arise at the first contact and take their concrete form over the course of weeks and months. Only then does it become visible what both may have already perceived at the first contact: a hint of fear, a rumbling in the stomach, a desire to direct and dominate her, or just a strange feeling that cannot be named. Something is not right. But what?

> "As a dog owner, you can observe this game very well. A dog is always dominated by another when it allows itself to be dominated. As soon as a bitch shows through her body language: 'Not like this!', sensitive bruisers immediately back off from the other. This does not require any barking or baring of teeth, it works just through the right body language."
> Dr. Angelika Weinländer Mölders, chemist, manager and co-editor of *Side by Side—Men at the Side of Successful Women*.

What starts inconspicuously in couple situations can escalate over time—the will to dominate, of one, and the ability to adapt, of the other. And from the will to dominate, expressed aggressions arise and from the ability to adapt, the urge to adapt in order to be loved or to be recommended for better jobs. Here, a fixation of the woman on her male counterpart takes place. And thus, predefined roles are fulfilled—welcome to the regiment of role attributions!

> Since patriarchal, dominating power always needs an opposite, it is indispensable not to offer oneself as an opposite anymore. The offering has two levels: stepping out of contact and/or dissolving an emotional fixation.

9.2 Exiting Power-Impotence Spirals

Depending on the situation, your personality and that of your male counterpart, I would like to give you some tools that can be used both in the job and in the private relationship. However, some of the strategies will not fully unfold their effect in the private relationship because you have a completely different closeness to the partner, physically and emotionally. A partner can also give much more space to his aggression in the private environment than he can do at the workplace.

This is about dealing with a negative, dominant power that ranges from power limitation to power abuse. The boundaries are fluid. How strongly the power-impotence spirals rotate, you can now co-determine. How you react to negative power exercise depends on several factors, including the type of power demonstration, the context in which it occurs, as well as your personality and that of your counterpart. The following tips are therefore of a general nature.

Physical Distance
Power seeks proximity. Whoever wants to exercise power needs people who let themselves be commanded—and are therefore within reach. And this means for women, first of all, to establish a physical distance.

For example, avoid physical proximity by no longer sitting directly opposite each other at meetings, but instead establishing a spatial distance within the seating arrangement. You should maintain this distance consistently: no extra conversation, no accidental meeting at the coffee machine. Make yourself scarce. Disappear from your boss's field of vision.

Body Language, Facial Expressions, Appearance, Voice: Not with me!
Power recognizes its victim. Anyone who signals submissiveness on a non-verbal level with body language, facial expressions, and appearance is perceived as a victim. You must counteract this. Start with your inner attitude and tell yourself: Not with me! An insecure, less confident

attitude becomes visible to the outside. You should stop tilting your head and smiling in the future, these are gestures of submission. In this way, you become more powerful and visibly leave your victim status. This makes you uninteresting for some power holders. The power game no longer works.

Reduction of Contacts

Power seeks control and lives from the number of contacts in which power can be lived out. So reduce contacts with power holders to a minimum, so that the control mechanism over you can no longer fully unfold its effect.

> "With a client, we outsmarted the boss's telephone control system by her calling him and giving a short, enthusiastic success report. 'Wow, it's that easy,' she was amazed, because within four weeks the control calls had been done, a meeting at the end of the week was enough."
> Marianne Brandt, coach and organizational developer.

Only participate in those meetings and events that are actually necessary and where your presence appears indispensable. Or leave the room during private discussions with the partner. Stand up and leave when you realize that you are not getting through with your arguments.

Reduction of Attention

Power always demands full attention. Reduce this bond of attention by, for example, changing the subject, interrupting monologues, or introducing other disruptive variables. Go to the toilet or make yourself a coffee. Disrupt his system.

Breaking Eye Contact or Fixation with Gaze

Power seeks eye contact, through which you are supposed to be controlled, or power avoids it, because through the control of eye contact, power is demonstrated. Both variants are possible.

Women tend to fixate on an opposite in order to hold on to the other's gaze or to ensure that they are seen. Thus, women are already subjugated through eye contact or also through the opposite of it, when power avoids it to irritate them.

> "When women look away or leaf through documents or—even worse—look interestedly at their fingernails while the boss is leading the meeting, they unsettle him. Nodding, smiling or tilting the head, on the other hand, are gestures of submission. They are not taken seriously with these." Marianne Brandt, coach and organizational developer.

You can easily counteract the game with eye contact by changing the seating arrangement. From now on: No meeting with a confrontational eye contact directly opposite.

Recognizing Patterns
Power operates in patterns. For example, aggression is followed by a conciliatory drink or the bedroom. Start questioning the patterns in which your aggressive, power-hungry partner or boss operates. You need to recognize the patterns in order to disrupt them. This means that if no sex follows a fight, you should also not signal a readiness to forgive. Aggressions should not be forgiven or excused.

Confronting Aggression
Power tolerates no contradiction. If you do not respond to power, or do not respond adequately, it means to your counterpart that they can extend their power even further. This means: Not responding or only half-heartedly responding to aggressions is grossly negligent! You need to prepare a repertoire of phrases that you have ready in case of an attack. Power renders women speechless. You need to find your language, only wisdom and accuracy can help in parrying: the right sentence at the right time! For example, you could say: "You don't talk to me like that! I expect a different tone."

Do Not Give Cause for Sexist Jokes
Power also operates through the expression of sexual fantasies. Therefore, never give cause for sexual remarks or even fantasies to be expressed in your presence, especially in the office. A skirt that is too

short, a neckline that is too deep at the after-work beer at the bar, both of you intoxicated, can make you the subject of conversation in such moments or afterwards. Stay formal in terms of your clothing, your handling of alcohol, or personal moments with colleagues and bosses.

Confident Handling of Mistakes

Power seeks points of attack, exploits weaknesses and fears—and looks for mistakes. One thing is clear: mistakes are not always avoidable. But German bosses usually have no culture of error. They will look for mistakes when they want to get rid of you. However, it would be bad advice to urgently avoid mistakes. Because mistakes are human. Strive for good work quality and confidently admit to mistakes when they happen. Sovereignty makes people strong, not weak. In case of a mistake, you could say, for example: "Unfortunately, I made a mistake because… I have learned from it and will take the insight into account next time."

Give the Other Person the Feeling That You Can Leave at Any Time

Power strives to possess people. It is all the more important to give the other person the feeling that you can leave at any time. You are not dependent on him, neither financially nor emotionally. Here you need to work on your attitude and your financial cushion.

A silent mantra in this regard could be: "I can manage well on my own—you, boss or man, are not worth me staying!"

Power Needs Resistance

Powerful people do not expect contradiction because they are too sure of their power.

Especially in strongly hierarchically structured companies or relationships that are traditionally patriarchal, power holders experience little contradiction from employees or partners. There are few clarifications, contradictions or counterarguments. To assert yourself, you need a clear message. A clarification that does not occur in a fight and not through long discussions, but is an unambiguous presentation of your position.

For example, you could say: "Based on my experience and competence, I can only say that I assess the situation differently." Make sure you don't get lost in long discussions. You won't win them. Because power does not think fact-based, but it is about demonstrating power.

Do Not Start Flirting and Do Not Allow It
Power seeks women who serve it. Flirting attempts in the boss's office make his life easier if he gets away with it because women feel upgraded. Refrain from that! Do not respond to it, nor start it yourself. This can become a relationship, but in many cases you will remain in the status of the mistress if your boss is married. The power imbalance between boss and employee is maintained.

Here it is important that you pay attention to your body language. Your inner attitude could be: I won't let you hit on me. What are you thinking? Your body will immediately switch to other body signals.

Outbursts of Anger: Leave the Room
Power carries anger within itself and strives to be lived out. In case of an outburst of anger, the only thing that helps is to leave the room or get up from the breakfast table. The only correct reaction: Stand up and leave! If outbursts of anger escalate, which they usually do when closeness has arisen, then only distance helps—possibly as a permanent separation or in the form of a termination. In psychology, we speak here of loss of impulse control. It is difficult to capture because control over oneself is lost. No arguments or conversation techniques help here. These losses of control repeat themselves, often triggered by certain triggers, often out of nowhere.

Negotiating with Your Own Fear
Power plays with your fear. It strives to hit you with your worst personal nightmares: loneliness, job loss, loss of status, existential fears… The fear it stirs up can be real or it is unreal and anticipated. This needs to be differentiated first. Which super-GAU could actually occur and hit you in a way that you actually experience a financial or emotional breakdown? If you can differentiate reality from unreal fears, you should

consider how you can confront these fears: What can help secure you so that you can survive termination or divorce well? And who can help?

We don't like our fears, they bother us. However, they are important helpers to draw our attention to inherited "baggage" and non-beneficial behaviors. It helps to take a closer look at fears. When you are no longer afraid of your fear, but understand how to use it for your benefit, you start to become free.

Do not attribute significance
Powerful women are a threat to male power, therefore they must be sanctioned. This is a risk you take. However, you only have this life and the question is whether you want to give the aggressively powerful partner or boss so much significance in your life. Because, if you stay, it also has something to do with the significance you attribute to the employer or partner. Perhaps your counterpart is not as significant for your life as you think. Power considers itself significant and often you adopt this belief unreflectively.

I wish for you to come to the realization: The most important thing in your life is you yourself and aggressively powerful people are not as relevant as you currently think. Stop attributing too much significance to these people. Only your attribution turns a negatively powerful person into an even more powerful person.

10

Conclusion

When women become powerful, the regime of role assignments loses its effect. Because it has long lived off male power and male self-confidence. To question the regime and even to withdraw from it requires reflection and resulting clarity as well as self-confidence and resulting courage. And this is on the part of women. True power comes from within. Externally, power works through status, money, and influence. But when the outside offers no opportunities for power, the key to gaining external power is the development of internal power.

We do not have a positive definition of power in our society. Power as a term is negatively connoted because power in a still patriarchally shaped system is also lived in a negative way—through abuse, violence, corruption, etc. To free ourselves from the regime of role assignments, we need to redefine power at the meta-level. This can only be achieved if we have more positive role models for power—not only on the men's side, but especially on the women's side. To put it simply: The concept of power must fall into good hands. If the much-heralded change of times is to bring about positive changes in the context of role assignments, more power must lie in female hands. The way to this initially leads via the internal development of power in the form of attitude, awareness, self-worth, and ego strength, and subsequently via more women in leadership and top positions.

Career begins with realization and self-empowerment. Knowledge is power. Power is based on attitude, strategies, negotiation skills, reflection, and proactive action. Power grows from the ability to recognize people's true motives and draw conclusions from them.

> "Career begins with becoming aware of your fears, feelings of guilt, and your shame, confronting them, distancing yourself from them, transforming them to overcome them. Because guilt, shame, and fear of women—for what and why actually?"

Career begins with the choice of partner and family planning. Career begins with the knowledge that the environment—partner, parents, circle of friends—pursues self-interests that need to be recognized. Career begins with putting oneself at the center. Career begins with realizing that we live in a violent society and that in companies as well as in partnerships, it is sometimes about keeping women small. Career begins with not persisting in such companies or such partnerships, out of misunderstood loyalty or fear of losing security. Career begins with realizing that you as a woman have power and can opt out. Or do you want to say at the end of your life what you have already heard from your mother and grandmother? Namely: "It was just like that, I couldn't do much."

I do not believe that laws are sufficient to bring more women into leadership positions or to implement equality as a value in our society. The current war in Ukraine shows that those who have power—due to weapons, fists, and dependencies—will also play out this power. And if the other side does not counteract this, it will be overrun. If women rely on legal regulations or on concessions from men, then they are sitting on their own pious wishes. The personalities of men are superior to women at the level of power and aggression due to millennia-old patriarchal structures, i.e. due to their role, their physiognomy, and their hormone status. And they use this superiority: privately, behind closed office doors, in closed circles, and subtly. Laws can only be a lever to change this.

Women themselves are called upon to take the scepter into their own hands. In other words: If you do not insist on your rights in your closest environment, both privately and professionally, if you belittle yourself and let yourself be belittled, then that is a decision that you have made, no one else!

The power of women begins with understanding all these connections, structures, and circumstances. And it unfolds through the assumption of personal responsibility—for one's own needs, goals, and desires, for one's own well-being, for one's own livelihood, and for one's own retirement provision. It is high time to get into action, to demand good conditions, and to exploit one's own potential, instead of exhausting oneself in the split between man, child(ren), and career. Discover your power! And at the center of power are you and no one else!

"It's not your job to exist for people and give them your life, bit by bit, moment by moment!"
Anthony Hopkins, Actor.

Addendum

Due to feedback on the book manuscript, I have found answers to questions that I had asked myself throughout the entire authorship, coaching, and interviewing activities, as well as during the psychological examination.

Test readers have noted that in the present book, I occasionally lack empathy for women—my analyses and conclusions are too negative, derogatory, or judgmental. It could be that some of my statements come across as "bashing". This initially deeply irritated me.

The specific request was: Have a little more compassion for women, they are under enormous expectations and pressure. By the way, this is also a role attribution! Compassion and empathy are among those qualities that are not only attributed to women, but also expected of them.

Intellectually, I can understand the arguments. However, I see the entire topic from a completely different perspective. Empathy helps to feel good in the short term. A nice vacation in the sun brings moments of happiness. When everyday life returns, the well-being quickly disappears again. So I decided to open a new perspective in this book: I want to confront you, make you think, and initiate change processes. But I am not aiming for a therapeutic process with this book by making you feel good while reading. My thesis is different: Change goes through pain, through confrontation with oneself and the other. This comes with unpleasant truths that initially appear negative. In addition, I probably reopen old wounds with some harsh statements. You may have had these injuries all your life, I just trigger them. I am your mirror.

Empathy does not solve the regime of role attributions. And it was noticeable that in the comments and remarks, little thought was given to dissolving role attributions. The comments end with women suffering from attributions—and then? Where is the solution? And if solution, it was, for example, on the company side.

For me, the solution lies in refusing attributions through more self-empowerment. Those who are powerful are less likely to surrender to attributions. What do I care about a daycare or other mothers who expect the cake for the children's party to be homemade? Do I really have to argue with my mother who thinks a full-time daycare is completely unhealthy for my child? Do I have to stay with an employer who doesn't want me as a mother?

Dear reader, why do you get the idea that you have to meet the expectations of others? The solution lies in distancing and turning away from the opinion or conviction of a counterpart who thinks in traditional role attributions. Refuse the societal dogma! In Germany and probably elsewhere, there is a tendency in public consciousness, which can be loosely formulated as: Feel with the women, then you are right. I would like to modify this credo: Show women a way to get out of their role attribution. This is also a form of empathy, but a more effective one than simple compassion. Because feeling with is nice, but it does not bring you closer to a solution for the prevailing regime of role attributions.

Glossary

Defense Mechanisms
Unconscious operations in which information is processed and kept away from consciousness to maintain psychological balance.

Fear-Violence Spirals
They arise from relationship constellations, the cohesion of which is fed by the fact that different protagonists remain in the system through the direct or indirect experience of open or subtle threats and the resulting fearful reactions, instead of actively and solution-orientedly confronting the actual threat. In this context, special variants can emerge, such as identification with the aggressor and consolidation of the prevailing system, avoidance and denial strategies, blame attributions towards those who need special protection. Instead of achieving a reduction of violence in the system through these forms of adaptive behavior, a spiral effect occurs, in which the intervals between violent interventions become shorter and their intensity increases. This phenomenon is more commonly known in the field of domestic violence.

Blind Spot
In psychology, the term blind spot refers to the tendency of people to ignore aspects of themselves that they cannot or do not want to perceive. Such people are essentially blind to certain characteristics or personality traits they possess, i.e., there is a difference between self-perception and the perception of others.

Double Messages/Double Binds
Contradictory verbal or non-verbal communications or messages that mutually exclude each other. This can involve messages where what is said and the manner of action do not match (preaching water and drinking wine yourself), or contradictory messages ("You are valuable to us as an employee." And: "In our company, everyone is replaceable."). Messages also act as double-edged when the inner emotional message does not match the external representation (for example: arms crossed and protective in front of the body with the message: "We can speak openly about everything with us."). Double messages put people in difficult situations. They must decide which message they can trust. Constantly used double binds can trigger psychosomatic complaints up to mental illnesses.

Dysfunctional Systems
Connections of people in which the relationships and communication behavior are disturbed. Fear, mistrust, and unpredictability characterize the atmosphere of dysfunctional systems.

Functional Systems
Connection of people, in which the relationships and communication behavior are characterized by an open, fear-free, and fact-based interaction in mutual respect.

Countertransference
The phenomenon of countertransference was first described by psychoanalysis in an interaction behavior of transference and countertransference between therapists and their patients. It is understood as a form

of transference in which a therapist responds to the patient (or to his actions and statements arising from transference phenomena) and in turn directs his own feelings, prejudices, expectations, and desires towards him. This phenomenon is now understood more broadly. In professional practice, people talk about transference relationships in which subjectively distorted perceptions of the other person occur. In this context, unconsciously acting experiences and expectations from one's own childhood can be the cause of the distorted reality perceptions.

Self-Identity
The totality of various self-images that enable people to distinguish themselves as individuals from others.

Ego Strength
The ego's ability to adapt to social reality and to process stress. People with a positively developed ego strength have a high self-esteem.

Codependency
Originally a term from addiction therapy. It refers to the entanglement of relatives with addicts. Today, the term is also applied to other dysfunctional relationship systems. Codependency describes a behavior of reference persons that contributes to minimizing or trivializing symptoms of dysfunctional behavior of others.

Compensation Strategy
In psychology, compensation is understood as the balance of a conscious or unconscious feeling of inferiority. Strategies are developed to achieve this balance of the feeling of inferiority. A planned compensation strategy could be, for example, that a stuttering person trains until he or she can give public speeches. Unconscious strategies can, for example, be shown in an authoritarian habitus, such as a particularly harsh and demonstrative treatment of employees, or also in status-enhancing behaviors such as the purchase of status goods or joining organizations with special prestige.

Congruence/Congruent Behavior
Alignment of nonverbal and verbal elements in communication. The body language is consistent with the content of a message as well as with the auditory sub-properties of the message.

Power-Impotence Systems
Relationship systems in which the assertion of individual or group self-interests predominates against the interest or will of others.

Parentification or Parentalization
A term from family therapy, which usually refers to a reversal of social roles between parents and their child.

Pseudo-Self-Strength
A high performance of the self in adapting to social reality and in processing stress is suggested. The self-esteem is not secured. A hidden self-weakness is compensated with a trained habitus of strength.

Reenactment
In psychoanalysis, it is referred to as "compulsion to repeat," which states that people often unconsciously create conditions that remind them of the original situation. In trauma research, it is assumed that reenactments represent attempts to cope with trauma.

Self-fulfilling Prophecy
Is a psychological phenomenon that can influence our own behavior, but also that of our fellow human beings. At its core, a self-fulfilling prophecy states: If we expect a certain behavior or outcome, we consciously or unconsciously contribute to this behavior or outcome actually occurring.

Self-Regulation
An umbrella term for abilities that allow people to consciously or unconsciously control their attention, emotions, impulses, and actions (self-control). Self-regulation includes, among other things, the mental

handling of one's own feelings and moods and the ability to realize intentions through purposeful and realistic actions (implementation strength or willpower).

Self-Denial
In psychoanalysis, denial is referred to as a defense mechanism that supports the splitting or also the splitting defense, thus the reactivation of an early childhood psychological state. The interplay of these two defense mechanisms results in negative aspects of the self or the environment not being integrated with the corresponding positive aspects. This mechanism is unconsciously set in motion to psychologically cope with difficult to bear experiences and events and at the same time to secure a right to exist in a communal context such as family, school, work, or friendships. One form of this coping and compensation mechanism is manifested in one's own devaluation and the denial of personal needs and legitimate claims.

Self-Worth
Also called self-esteem, it is the evaluation of the image of oneself (self-concept) and thus a fundamental attitude towards one's own person.

Stimuli
Stimuli for activating behavior. Stimuli can be distinguished into emotional stimuli (emotionally emphasized), cognitive stimuli (thought emphasized), and physical (physical) stimuli (perception emphasized).

Transgenerational Transmission
Usually unintentional, often unconscious, and not infrequently also unwanted events and traumas, against the background of which the experiences of the members of one generation are transmitted to the members of subsequent generations.

Twisting
A manipulation technique through which assumptions are anchored as realities.

Sources
https://de.wikipedia.org/
https://entwicklung-der-persoenlichkeit.de/
https://karrierebibel.de/
https://lexikon.stangl.eu/
https://wirtschaftslexikon.gabler.de
http://www.diagnose-gewalt.eu/
https://www.spektrum.de/lexikon/psychologie/

Book Recommendations

Transgenerational Transmissions

Baer, U.; Frick-Baer, G.: How Traumas Affect the Next Generation: Investigations, Experiences, Therapeutic Aids. Samnos, 2010.
Bode, Sabine: "Traces of War: The German Disease German Angst", 2016.
Huber, Michaela; Plassmann, Reinhard: Transgenerational Traumatization, Junfermann Publishing, 2012.
Moré, Angela: "The Unconscious Transmission of Traumas and Guilt Entanglements to Subsequent Generations", In: Journal for Psychology, Vol. 21 (2013), Issue 2.
Mitscherlich, Alexander and Margarete: "The Inability to Mourn: Foundations of Collective Behavior", Munich, 1967.
Opher-Cohn, L.; Pfäfflin, J.; Sonntag, B.; Klose, B.; Pogany-Wnendt, P. (Eds.): "The End of Speechlessness? Effects of Traumatic Holocaust Experiences Over Several Generations." edition psychosocial, 2000.
Proesl, Ulrike: "Genograms in Business Coaching", Books On Demand, 2020.
Welsch, Wolfgang: "My Resistance Against the SED State", Conversations with Contemporary Witnesses, DVD, 95 min., OEZ Publishing Berlin.
Radebold, H.; Bohleber, W.; Zinnecker, J. (Eds.): "Transgenerational Transmission of War-Burdened Childhoods. Interdisciplinary Studies on

the Sustainability of Historical Experiences Over Four Generations." JUVENTA, 2008.

Welsch, Wolfgang: "The Sting of the Scorpion—On the Stasi's Death List" based on the experiences of Wolfgang Welsch, DVD, Studio Hamburg, 2007.

Functional/Dysfunctional Family Constellations

https://www.businessinsider.de/karriere/arbeitsleben/kinder-brauchen-bedinungslose-liebe-2018-6/
https://www.selbsthilfehelden.com/dysfunktionale-familien-10-merkmale
Bode, Sabine: "Traces of War: The German Disease German Angst", 2016
Hickey, Birgit: "How the Family Determines Our Life. Genogram and Systemic Constellations." Carl Auer, 2022
Tomann, Walter: "Family Constellations: Their Influence on the Individual", C.H.Beck, 2020

Self-Worth/Self-Strength

Chmielewski, Fabian; Hanning, Sven: "Therapy Tools Self-Worth, With E-Book inside and Working Material", Beltz, 2021 (Set with various articles)
Online Encyclopedia for Psychology and Pedagogy, Topic Self-Strength, 3rd Definition according to Köck Ott, 1994, p. 310 and Stangl, 2020.
Potreck, Friederike; Jacob, Gitta: "Self-Attention, Self-Acceptance, Self-Confidence. Psychotherapeutic Interventions for Building Self-Esteem" (Life Learning, Vol. 163), Klett Cotta, 2016

Couple Relationship

Asendorpf, Jens; Banse, Reiner: "Psychology of the Relationship", Hans Huber Publishing, 2000
Conin-Ohnsorge/Lackner/Weinländer-Mölders, Men at the side of successful women: Side by Side to the top, 1st edition, Haufe-Lexware, 2018

Kaiser, Peter: "Partnership and Couple Therapy", Hogrefe Publishing, 2000
Schindler, Ludwig: "Partnership problems?: How to make your relationship work—Handbook for couples", Springer Publishing, 2020

Attachment Theory

Brisch, Karl Heinz: "Trauma and Attachment Across Generations. Inherited Wounds and Resilience in Therapy, Counseling and Prevention, Latest Findings from the Field of Epigenetics, Resilience Research, Prevention and Trauma Therapy", Klett Cotta, 2022
Brisch, Karl Heinz: "Attachment and Mental Disorders. Causes, Treatment and Prevention", Klett Cotta, 2021

Motherhood and Career

Buckels, E. E., Jones, D. N., & Paulhus, D. L. (2013). Behavioral Confirmation of Everyday Sadism. Psychological Science, 24(11), 2201–2209. https://doi.org/10.1177/0956797613490749 In: https://www.sueddeutsche.de/wissen/psychologie-der-sadist-unter-uns-1.1799935
Rieder, Peter: „Study: Part-time job/Part-time employment: Are part-time workers more efficient and capable?", commissioned by Arbeitswelten Consulting and Family & Career Management, University of Applied Sciences Vienna, https://www.hrweb.at/2017/03/teilzeitjob-teilzeitbeschaeftigung-studie/
https://www.dw.com/de/das-einfrieren-von-eizellen-geht-aufs-haus/a-17999952

Power

Bauer-Jelinek, Christine: "The bright and the dark side of power: How to achieve your goals without betraying your values", ecowin, November 13, 2020
Knaths, Marion: "Playing with power: How women assert themselves", Pieper Verlag, 2009

For readers who are looking for a sparring partner to work through personal issues, I recommend the following points of contact

- Consult your general practitioner if you want to seek therapeutic help. He or she will explain the next steps to you.
- Contact the Psychotherapist Chamber of your federal state. It is the professional representation for practicing therapists and can provide you with contact details of therapists in your area.
- The National Association of Statutory Health Insurance Physicians (kbv.de) provides a nationwide and regional overview of doctors, psychotherapists, and psychiatrists. It also provides information.

GPSR Compliance

The European Union's (EU) General Product Safety Regulation (GPSR) is a set of rules that requires consumer products to be safe and our obligations to ensure this.

If you have any concerns about our products, you can contact us on

ProductSafety@springernature.com

In case Publisher is established outside the EU, the EU authorized representative is:

Springer Nature Customer Service Center GmbH
Europaplatz 3
69115 Heidelberg, Germany

www.ingramcontent.com/pod-product-compliance
Lightning Source LLC
LaVergne TN
LVHW050013270326
834688LV00069B/106